Alfred The Great and:
The Army of the Hardway Road

J J Harlow

Grosvenor House
Publishing Limited

This book is published by
Grosvenor House Publishing Ltd
Link House
140 The Broadway, Tolworth, Surrey, KT6 7HT.
www.grosvenorhousepublishing.co.uk

A CIP record for this book
is available from the British Library

ISBN 978-1-83615-228-6
eBook ISBN 978-1-83615-229-3

My Thanks To Anny,
For the delightful artwork.

The Old Kingdoms

scotland

northumbria

North Sea

Isle of Man

Irish Sea

mercia

east anglia

wales

wessex

cornwall

Isle of Wight

Introduction.

In my view, there were two moments which defined England as a nation. The first was with Alfred the Great, and the victory over the Vikings at Edington in 878. That was – for all practical purposes – the moment when England first got going. That was the transitionary phase from a collection of tribal groupings, to a coalescence around a singular point.

The second phase of the nation state development occurred hundreds of years later, when the parliamentary forces under the gentleman farmer Cromwell, defeated the forces of iniquitous deification as represented by Charles the first. It was here that the old feudal mind-set was superficially put to one side. It was a mind-set which had previously seen all the land within a certain geographical boundary as – not a nation state – but as the private country estate of a monarch who believed themselves to be a deity here on earth.

The legal primacy of Parliament – which had its roots in Magna Carta – set in concrete the notion that England was not some plaything to be swopped about as the fancy took them, by regal nonentities with a God complex; but was in fact a coalition of broadly like-minded people, who had an equality of opinion regarding the environment they shared. (In theory at least).

This book is focused on the people of that ancient time. They were the people of the Hardway Road. The Hardway, being the name of the ancient road which farmers and working people travelled up and down in the bitter war against the Viking invaders. These ordinary working people formed the Army of The Hardway Road. It was the first English Army. It was a volunteer army. It was the people's army. No conscripts. Just ordinary folk – freedom fighters – leaving their farms and places of work to come together in a common cause against the Viking globalists.

When people join together under difficult circumstances in a shared cause, it can't but elevate that cause onto a higher spiritual plane. We have seen that collective gathering throughout history. It is a potent force. The English are the definitive people of the Hardway Road; but it would be churlish to deny that throughout history, there is not a corner of the world where the oppressed and the down trodden have not also walked a Hardway Road.

They must tell their own story, and it is one that resonates with me when they do. I may be an Englishman, but I believe that we are all connected.

This however, is the English story and its beginnings. It's not about the colour of your skin; your religion; your ethnic background; or any other faux political aesthetic you use to promote some, faux in the moment political dogma. It is about you the person. That spiritual part of you and how it interacts with those around you.

A time long ago,
He travelled the Hardway Road.
His name was Alfred.

On The Hardway Road.

Met fierce in green fields,
Trampled muddy and red.
Where the force of an English river,
Long and wide.
Meets the boiling rush,
Of an incoming tide.

Long struggles join,
In close contested maul;
And proudly worn,
Viking high helmets,
Ring with a muted peal.
Under the bell hammer toll,
Of hard English steel.

Dark oaths exchanged,
As pell mell, greets melee.
Where the sum of a man,
Is in the shared common load;
And the company he keeps,
On the Hardway Road.

Some Quick Facts To Get you Started.

1. Alfred The Great was the first democratically elected King. There were no ballot papers in those days; no polling booths; no dodgy postal votes from the recently departed. People voted with their feet. They left their farms and families to join with a King and put their very existence on the line in a cause they believed in. You don't get more democratic than that.

2. Alfred was the world's first Mandela. Like Nelson Mandela – the man he preceded by over a thousand years – he was essentially a man of peace, whose preference in life was for scholarly pursuits. But when events moved Alfred onto the field of battle, he was of necessity, an uncompromising brute.

3. Alfred was also England's first and greatest Patriotic Socialist. He was in nature and style little different to the working class men and women who were the backbone of the Labour Party, which came to power in the aftermath of the Second World War. Like them, he was a patriot who put his life on the line in the fight against a determined foe. The similarities between Alfred and those who joined and formed the post war Labour Government are numerous. In his own post war period he also implemented reforms which saw an uplift in all areas of English life. The scope of his achievements were quite remarkable. But don't expect the upper middle class pretend socialists who control the modern day Labour Party to sing his praises or erect statues in his honour. That is because they have absolutely nothing in common with working people like Alfred. In fact, they quietly despise them. Alfred was nothing like them. Alfred was a man true of heart. A man prepared to stand shoulder to shoulder with his comrades in their darkest hour. Alfred was a real socialist; a bona fide patriot and liberal by disposition. Alfred was of the people; with the people; and for the people. From a Patriotic Socialist perspective: Alfred was the real deal.

4. Alfred's wife Ealhswith, was the first English feminist. He was King of England, but she wasn't crowned Queen. I have to say,

I very much like that idea. She wasn't defined by her husband's status. Not for her the phony entitlement of a status bestowed upon her, because she happened to take the eye of a gold plated nob, who took her to his bed chamber and impregnated her with his regal sceptre. Ealhswith was a person in her own right.

5. The Army of the Hardway Road was the first English Army. It takes its name from the Hardway Road (often known as the Harrow Way; and perhaps more of a track than a road) along which the farmers and labourers who made up the army, gathered and marched. As much as a fighting force, it was a state of mind. It was born of a contradiction: You have to fight to be left in peace.

6. Aethelflaed was Alfred's oldest girl and oldest child. (He had 5 children. 2 boys and 3 girls). Her husband Aethelred, Lord of the Mercians, died in in 911. After his death, she became Myrcna Hlaefdige (Lady of the Mercians) and took up arms and led her troops to battle where she promptly set about kicking Viking butt. In common with the women of her time, she was tough as old boots, and like her mum, she was a feminist in the truest sense of the word, even when the word itself had yet to come into existence.

7. The 'True Heart' is the name of the spiritual battle flag of England. Its name is a reflection of the disposition of the ordinary folk who without force or coercion, put their lives on the line and walked together as equals, along The Hardway Road.

8. The number 8 is the spiritual number of the English. Eight is the number of stars on the spiritual battle flag of the Army of The Hardway Road. The stars themselves represent the gestation period during which the English nation was formed. The word, 'Hardway,' has a numerological value of eight; as does the flags name: 'True Heart.' The number eight represents infinity. This is an appropriate value as the English – more than most – have been subject to stress through invasive wars from close neighbours; but still they go on. (For those unfamiliar with the term: Numerology is an esoteric science whereby you ascribe numbers to dates, letters, words or names, in order to divine the future or gain spiritual insight into the personality behind those words).

9. The word 'Angelcynn,' is the ancient word for 'English.' Cynn, (pronounced chin) means people (or tribe). Angel, in its modern context, means: 'a benevolent celestial being.' So essentially, the English are: the People of the Angels. (So that's alright then. So move along folks. Nothing more to discuss here).

10. The rose may be the flower of England, but the carnation is the flower of the Hardway Road.

11. As previously stated, Alfred was very much the man of peace, but on the battlefield he did what all great warriors do. In the heat of battle, when the fighting is at its fiercest, they go deep into their soul and call upon their inner 'Dickie Plantagenet.' There was no person or group of people more ferocious than the Plantagenets. So the fact that Alfred was able to 'Out Dickie,' Richard Plantagenet and his 'fruges ili' (fruits of the loin), was some achievement. The fact he got his 'Dickie P' on, almost 300 hundred years before the Plantagenets arrived on the scene, is a further demonstration that Alfred was indeed a man ahead of his time.

12. Alfred was also something of a polymath. For those who don't know what a polymath is: it is someone with a broad knowledge and skill set. Someone able to turn their hand to many a varied and challenging task. It is a wonderful talent to possess. I myself am also something of a polymath – as evidenced by this scholastic tome, with its sprinkling of intellectual stardust, wrapped gorgeously in a potpourri of neuron friendly ruminations.

13. Alfred's father was Aethelwulf, which in old English means: 'the noble wolf.' Given his bloodline, it is hardly surprising therefore, that Alfred was able to bring those Viking mutts to heel. Even in those days – and well before it became part of current street slang – you don't mess with the big dog!

14. Unlike the semantically elegant Alfred, Charlemagne (Charles the Great of France) was illiterate throughout his Kingly career. Charlemagne could barely read or write. So amongst the 'Greats' of the early European middle ages, Alfred was indisputably a bard amongst Greats; and unlike Shakespeare – who perhaps would go on to become the greatest Bard, England has ever produced – Alfred achieved his brand of learned

bardship whilst bearing the fardels and pressures of early nationhood. Whom amongst us I wonder, could bear such fardels against a sea of Viking troubles and by opposing, end them? Certainly not Charles the faux manger, who wouldn't know his Bottom from his Banquo.

The True Heart.

The True Heart is the spiritual battle flag of the Hardway Road, and by extension, the spiritual battle flag of England.

It is composed of a red heart shaped motif which sits at the very centre of the flag. A continuous thin white line delineates the edge. The heart sits within a blue oblong design.

The remainder of the flag shows a red background, punctuated by eight five pointed stars. Each star point is representative of Alfred and his four brothers, who were to the fore in the fight against the Foul Viking Globalists. Looking from left to right, four stars sit above the blue oblong design and four stars sit below.

The eight stars represent the gestation period when England was being formed. This is taken as the years 871 to 878 inclusive. 871 was when Alfred succeeded his brother Aethelred, who had died shortly after the battle of Ashdown. The year 878 was when Alfred emerged from his retreat at Athelney and marched with his army along the Hardway Road to Edington, whereupon he delivered unto Guthren and his Viking convocation the bitter fruits of a necessary defeat.

The colours are symbolic: The red and white symbolize the undeniable commonality that exists between human beings. It is a part of human psychology that we over accentuate the physical differences that exist between us, and then having done that, incorporate those – often mendacious observations – into our social political thinking. The differences become our credo. The differences include, skin colour; age; ethnicity; religion; cultural background; financial resources; even differences of view which exist within the followers of the same religion or sect; etc.

The red symbolizes the colour of our blood, and the white the colour of our bones. This is appropriate, because a flag should be a representation of all the people. So scratch the surface and we are all the same under the skin. We are all connected. We are as one.

The blue is for the sky above. In those moments of quiet contemplation, when we seek answers which lay beyond our physical realm, we tend to look upwards. The blue is for those moments.

The heart motif speaks for itself. It is a physical symbol which combines the emotive mix of life, hope, and the will to endure.

Those volunteers who walked with Alfred along the Hardway, towards a future which might see their lives brought to a bloody end, were the True Hearts in every sense of the word. They didn't have to be there. They could have gone into hiding and ignored the call to battle. They could have kept their heads down. But the true heart will put itself in harm's way for the greater good. That's not just an English trait, exclusive unto those within this small island, it is a human one. I think a flag, whilst pointing to the geo social group from which it emerged, should also have the spiritual qualities which allows those outside the group to identify with it as well.

The True Heart is saying to the world, 'this is us and we are you.'

> The dove is in love,
> Upon a tall tree he sits.
> He sings a high coo.

Numerology and The True Heart of The Hardway.

For those unfamiliar with the subject: numerology is the study of numbers and the way they interact on a human level in our lives. At first glance, it may seem that Numerology is a form of mathematics which operates in a similar fashion to the techniques employed in statistical analysis.

Numerology isn't quite like that. It operates more in a mystical, spiritual sphere. It suggests that numbers have an intrinsic personality which both predict and reflect, what we might describe as, 'the mood music' elements of an individual's character, and in doing so offer guidance regarding the direction of travel.

It operates on a practical level by applying numerical values to the letters of the alphabet and using the resulting sum as a means to offer insight into a spiritual intangible. It is a study which has been practised for thousands of years and is evident in many cultures and religions.

Like many things, the results are open to interpretation and the manner in which you apply the attributes.

How it works: In Pythagorean numerology, each letter of the alphabet is assigned a number from one through to nine as shown.

1	2	3	4	5	6	7	8	9
A	B	C	D	E	F	G	H	I
J	K	L	M	N	O	P	Q	R
S	T	U	V	W	X	Y	Z	

To calculate the numerological value of the word, **'Hardway,'** is as follows:

8h + 1a +9r +4d +5w +1a +7y = 35

Then, except when the sum total comes to 11 or 22, **you add the 3 and 5 together which produces 8.**

In numerology, the numbers one to nine and numbers eleven and twenty two, all have a personality meaning. (Eleven and twenty two are said to be, **master numbers**. Eleven is regarded as a masculine number, suggesting strength; and twenty two as a feminine number, which suggests an intuitive bias).

So when analysing the personality meaning of the name, **'Hardway,'** you could say that the 8h+1a+9r+4d+5w+1a+7y = 3+5 is the spiritual dna of the word. Examination of the dna, offers a basis for noting certain inherent traits, and thereby suggesting a direction of travel.

The spiritual **dna** number of **'Hardway,'** is **8**.

This is an interesting number. The number is perfectly symmetrical and represents cosmic balance. When turned on its side it is the symbol for infinity. It goes on without end. It exists in all places and at all times. Amongst its key attributes, are a sense of imagination and purpose. From a positive aspect, it denotes, strength, leadership, the ability to endure. It offers a sense of the karmic balance which sits between the heavenly divine and earth's more prosaic demands.

On the negative side it may – if left unchecked – reveal an over ambition which might steer it away from its karmic equipoise towards a more intolerant disposition. The rebellious part of its nature, which is of great value when fighting Tory injustice, can – if misdirected – move the compass reading towards such negatives as intolerance and authoritative behaviour.

Notwithstanding the negatives, the number 8, starts in a beautiful place. It stands perfectly in cosmic balance. It is at one with the Universe. Like a child brought up in a healthy nurturing environment, it is equipped with all the tools required to lead a full and productive life. But as in all human experience, it is the manner in which those tools are employed, that will ultimately prove crucial.

So we have the name, 'Hardway,' which has a numerological (dna) value of eight.

The name of the spiritual battle flag of the Army of the Hardway Road is: **True Heart.**

The personality **dna** number of **'True Heart,'** is also **eight**.

The flag itself has eight stars. Each star representing the gestation year when England was being formed.

Four stars are in line above the heart symbol and four below. The two groups are in symmetrical balance, like the number 8 itself.

The flag can be described as a: **'red heart and eight stars.'** This description has a numerological **dna of 8**.

The letter **'H'** which is the start of, **'Hardway,'** is the eighth letter of the alphabet. So the letter **'H'** also has a **dna value of 8**.

The animal totem of Hardway, is the Phoenix. The Phoenix is an ancient symbol of rebirth. From out of the flames of destruction, a new life emerges. This is quite symbolic, as at the beginning of the march along the Hardway, England was a ruin, and the legend of Alfred burning the cakes has become a metaphor for a nation consumed in fire. The end of the Hardway, saw a nation born out of fire; both literally and allegorically. (Also of interest to note: we don't know the exact date Alfred was born, but he died on 26th October 899. There are a number of animals which – from an astrological perspective – sit within this star sign, but one of them is the Phoenix. So there is a curious linkage there).

Other names which share the number eight in their dna are: God; spiritual; religion; prophet; Torah; Moses; Abraham; womb; temple; karma; creator; eternity; sanctum sanctorum, (which means the holy of holies). So the people of the Hardway and the flag that is their visual representation, share their numerological dna with some inspiring words.

People may be interested to note that the master numbers, eleven and twenty two, are held by amongst others:

Jesus and Muhammad, who both share master number eleven.

Also at master number 11 is, United Kingdom.

Also at master number 11 are, the combined words: England, Scotland, Northern Ireland, Wales.

Also at Master number 11: London.

Other Number 11's include: Beijing; Buenos Aires; Riyadh, Kabul; and Hanoi.

Words which are not master numbers include: European Union; Paris; Berlin; Brussels; Strasbourg; Washington; Tokyo; Moscow; Davos; and the 'World Economic Forum.'

And, 'Buddha' which has a name with the master number, twenty two.

Also at 22 is (the capital of Greece) Athens (and the capital of Poland) Warsaw.

So the Master capital cities of the world are at numbers 11 and 22.

Though it must be said that we who have travelled the Hardway, are proud to embrace our brothers and sisters in Lisbon, Dublin, Riga and Istanbul, whom share with us, the numerological **dna 8**.

Attributes and Personality Traits of Life Numbers:
(Both the Positives and the Negatives)

1. (Number 1, is associated with God, as after this, all other numbers were created). Leadership; individual; proactive; self-sufficient; innovative; forceful; a focused view point which can at times, result in narrow mindedness. (Note: The word, 'man,' has a numerological value of 1).
2. Balanced; the yin to number ones yang; intuitive; diplomatic; empathetic; but can be indecisive.
3. Expressive; sociable; a good communicator; creative; naïve, but sometimes lacking focus. (Note: The word, 'woman' has a numerological value of 3).
4. Dependable; conservative; hardworking; steady; at times dogmatic; can be inflexible.
5. Visionary; independent; curious; goes with the flow; may sometimes lack commitment.
6. Responsible; nurturing; romantic; nurturing; passive; at times impractical.
7. Understanding; spiritual; curious; logical; suspicious; can be inward looking.
8. Practical; strong; power seeking; eternal; an achiever; balanced; thrives best in a karmic environment; quietly determined; can be over authoritative when its karmic balance is not centred; may ignores rules (not always a bad thing).
9. Humanitarian; creative; compassionate; tolerant; romantic; supportive; likes to be liked; might be lacking in self-analysis.
11. Spirituality; idealism; intuitive; inspirational.
22. The Master builder; power; methodical.

Note: The Master numbers have the capacity to bring about both intolerable hardship or lead to higher planes of health and good fortune. It will often be one or the other.

It is interesting to note that the name, 'Alfred,' falls within life number one; which of course has leadership as its primary attribute.

Other words in this category include: Saxon; Boudica; Parliament and Winston Churchill.

It is also worth noting that the name Alfred, is attributed to the plant spirit Carnation. So for those of us who have spent the greater part of our existence walking life's Hardway, let it be known that our number is eight; the Phoenix our indestructible spirit totem; the True Heart a symbol of our communal allegiance, and inspired by the aesthetic beauty of the carnation, shall our dreams come to flower.

Note: Humans are a mixture of differing personality traits. It is the manner in which those traits are mixed and the quantities at which they are present which will determine the eventual outcome. You can think of it as the ingredients of a cake. The same ingredients can produce completely different results. Those finished results can range from the sublimely delightful, to the inedible sick maker. Too much flour and too little milk and butter will produce a dry paste. Too much butter will produce a greasy lump. The perfect ingredients mixed in the perfect proportions, will result in perfection. Also, the cooking process can be used as a metaphor for the environment in which a person is brought up in. That will affect the ingredients in either a generally positive or generally negative fashion. A poor environment will most likely accentuate certain negative traits, while leaving the positives ones, somewhat underdeveloped.

For those readers – many of whom may not be familiar with the subject – there are many websites which explain numerology in finer detail. Additionally, there are many websites which have a numerology calculator which allows you to enter the name or word which is of interest, and it will do the calculations for you. One such website is:

https://www.thecalculator.co/ (Once there, look for the section: Calculator by Name).

This is a useful site, as it has a lot of different calculators ranging from calculators to evaluate how racist you are, to whether you are schizophrenic.

I took both tests, and you will be pleased to learn that I am neither racist nor schizophrenic. Which didn't come as a surprise, because had I been either of these, then the voices in my head would have told me; and it is worth pointing out that one of those voices belongs to the eminent psychiatrist Sir Rodney Nut Nut; who scored a double first in psychology, at Cuckoo College, Boo Boo Land.

There is no doubt that numerology does throw up some interesting patterns. As mentioned before, if you put into the calculator England 3, Scotland 7, Wales 6, Northern Ireland 4, on an individual basis, then each home nation has a different numerological dna. But if you put all four names into the calculator together, (as if they were one word or sentence) then the result is, Master Number 11.

Coincidentally, if you put the words English 11, Scottish 5, Welsh 22, Irish 9 into the calculator, then even though their individual numbers are all different, they collectively produce the Master number 11. (And kudos to the English and Welsh for their individual Master Number scores).

To add to the ongoing Numerological coincidence: if you put the word, 'United Kingdom,' into the calculator, then you also get, Master Number 11. So, in numerological terms, the sum of the four home nations = United Kingdom.

Also at number eleven is, 'Downing Street.'

Parliament and House of Commons are both at number one.

Other interesting anomalies: J K Rowling 11; Harry Potter 11; Ron Weasley 11; Hagrid 11; Severus Snape 11; Lord Voldemort 11; Muggle 11. Given the repetition of the master number 11, it's almost as if there is something magical going on there.

In footballing terms, a number of English clubs in the Premier League score ones, eights and elevens. More so than might at first glance appear statistically probable.

Manchester United 8. Red Devils 8. Old Trafford 11.

Law, Charlton, Best, 11.

Manchester City 1. The Cityzens 1. Pep Guardiola 8; Maine Road 8; Sheikh Mansour 8: Etihad Stadium 8; The Blues 11; Blue Moon Rising 11; Etihad 11; The Poznan 11; Kevin de Bruyne 11.

Bell, Summerbee, Lee, 1.

Reds v Blues, 1

The Manchester City home match against Real Madrid on Wednesday 17th May 2023 in the champions League, in which City won four nil and was described by many, as the best performance by the club ever. I didn't actually witness the game, but as a matter of interest I put the City starting line up into the calculator: Ederson Santana de Moraes; Kyle Walker; Ruben Dias; Manuel Akanji; Ilkay Gundogan; Kevin de Bruyne; John Stones; Rodri Hernandez Cascante; Erling Haaland; Jack Grealish; Bernardo Silva. The result came out as Master Number 11.

On a technical note: Perhaps one of the reasons that Manchester City have enjoyed so much success under their manager, **Pep Guardiola,** (peoples dna number, 8) is because he has a style of play which mimics the rhythmic style of the iambic pentameter, which was a favourite of the great English bard, William Shakespeare. (Note: 'iambic pentameter' has a dna of 1).

This can be observed via the rhythmic precision of how a Bard Guardiola team usually plays. (Assuming all components are fully fit and not mentally knackered).

Con-Trol, and Pass. Re-Ceive and Go; Re-Peat. (The entire concept is: dna master number, 11).

And of course, within Manchester City's stylistic core, are delightful metaphors and poetic subtexts, all held together in a mellifluous embrace. All very Shakespearean. All displaying, that harmonic periodicity, commonly referred to as, 'poetry in motion.'

For those unfamiliar with the term, 'iambic pentameter:' it is a rhythmic structure within the written word, which poets have employed for thousands of years, whose tempo mimics the rhythm of the beating heart. It contains 5 pairs of stressed and unstressed syllables, making 10 outfield playing syllables in total. Shakespeare absolutely loved a iambic pentameter; and it would appear that Bard Guardiola does to. (Also Worth Noting: In the Chinese Zodiac, Manchester City were born under the sign of the Metal Dragon. (Metal, being their element). Manchester United, under the sign of the Tiger. Liverpool, the Dragon, and Everton, the Tiger).

So perhaps when they are finalising their team selection, football managers need to consider, not only how it all looks from a Numerological perspective, but how it's shaping up from an iambic one.

Some other footballing numerologies:

'The F.A.' 22; Fifa, 22; Football, 11; Futbol, 22; and, Goal, 8.

Continuing on a football theme, I had a look at the football World Cup from its inception in 1930 to the present day. In particular, I focused on the actual year when the tournament was played and the winner in each year.

Numerological fans might be interested to learn that England won the competition in 1966. This is not new information, however what will be new, is the fact that if you add up the numbers: one plus nine, plus six, plus six; you get, **Master Number 22.**

The only other Master number victory to occur in the competition, is in 2018, when the French were victorious. (Two plus zero, plus one, plus eight = **Master number 11**).

I found this both interesting and reassuring, because of all the nations on earth which are most suited to achieve footballing success in a Master Number year, then you could not pick any two finer examples.

I say this because, with most nations the Master Number accolade would go straight to their head. It will intoxicate them. They will become completely insufferable. They will strike a pose which is at once, both haughty and arrogant. A personality trait which is completely alien to both the French and English. So the fact that of all the choices available, that only these two were nominated as the supreme footballing chosen ones, suggests to me that there is a divine force at work in the Universe. Some unseen hand which is moving in a mysterious way. It is a very comforting thought.

Moving the numerological debate away from football and into the unsullied waters of British politics:

We can now see that of the UK political Parties, that Reform UK punches a lot of interesting numbers. Reform UK 8; The Reform Party 8; Reform Party 11.

With regard to Reform UK, it is worth noting that their leader Mr. Nigel Farage, tried and failed on 7 separate occasions to get elected to Parliament. It was only at the eighth attempt that he succeeded.

Also his first grandchild was born on the eighth anniversary of Brexit. Also their deputy leader is Richard Tice. His name – **Richard Tice** – has a dna of **8**. First chairman, **Zia Yusuf,** has a dna of, **Master number 11**. (The same as **Jesus and Muhammad**). They style themselves as: The People's Army. **'People's Army,'** has a dna of 1; and, **'Vote Reform,'** is at: **Master Number 11.**

Politics is a very divisive subject, but whether you like it or not – in numerological terms – Reform UK, are fighting for the people; and in terms of their spiritual dna, can lay claim to the honorific, **'People's Champion.'**

To offer some political balance, I would mention also that the official name of the Welsh political Party, **'Plaid Cymru'** is: **'Plaid Cymru – The Party of Wales.'** This has a dna of 1. Also if you write their official name in the Welsh language you get:

'Plaid Cymru - Eich Plaid Leol Chi.' This also has a dna value of 1. So as an Englishman who has been blessed with having a lot of lovely Welsh people in his life, I'm pleased that the Party of Wales can make a claim for the number one spot.

(Note: Plaid Cymru - Eich Plaid Leol Chi, translates into English as: Plaid Cymru – Your Local Party).

(On a separate issue – which may or may not be relevant – it is also worth noting, that in terms of the Chinese Zodiac, that the main Party leaders who contested the 2024 General Election, were: Nigel Farage (Reform) who was born under the sign of the Dragon. Sir Keir Starmer (Labour) who was born under the sign of the Tiger. Sir Ed Davy, the leader of the Liberal Democrats, who was born under the sign of the Snake; and Rishi Sunak, who was a Rat).

Not being an expert in statistical analysis, I am unable to quantify how expected or unusual the numerological dna's recorded here are. There were certainly a number of themes which kept repeating themselves. Too many – which to my mind – fell outside the remit of simple coincidence; and I can assure you that there were a lot more examples of this repetitious behaviour than I have published here. I mean, if you take the fact that so many of the characters from Harry Potter score a dna value of Master Number 11, then that certainly offers pause for thought.

Though, in writing this section I am also mindful of the suggestion which hypothecates that anything is possible, as evidenced by the idea, that if you gave an infinite number of monkeys an infinite number of typewriters and an infinite amount of time, then eventually, they will type out the collected works of Shakespeare. So it may be that the numerological examples I have given here, aren't strange at all. Perhaps they are operating in a statistically predictable range. Simply a case of, 'move along you statistical anomalies, there is nothing anomalous to see here.'

In bringing this section to a close, I would say it is up to you to decide how much weight you wish to attach to the subject. Though

I am sure a lot of you will enjoy putting different words into the calculator and checking the results.

In any event, I think you'll agree that we have learnt a lot of new things in this section:

We learnt that Numerology is a fascinating subject.

We learnt that the French and English are neither haughty nor arrogant.

We learnt that the Chinese Zodiac can produce winners (Dragons) and losers (Rats).

We learnt that eight is the peoples number.

But most of all, we learnt that Shakespeare was a monkey.

Once Upon A Time Before England.

Once the ice age receded, there was a general migration from warmer climes towards the cooler north. This migration occurred in approximately 10,000 BC. First Mesolithic Hunter-Gatherers, then following on from them at around 4,000 BC, Neolithic farmers, from regions like the Rhine Valley and the Low counties.

Iron Age Celtic tribes followed, beginning around 800 BC. But, given the geographical disposition of England in relation to Wales, Scotland and Ireland, then it is correct to say that these Celtic people would have arrived on 'English' soil, first.

So clearly this means that the English were the first Celtics. Which in turn means that they are more Celtic than their good neighbour chums in Scotland, Wales and Ireland.

So in the **'Celtic Ordo Descendit,'** (Celtic Order descending):

England are: **'Celtic Tribe A.O.K. Number One.'**

Which in Latin is: **'Celtic Tribus A.O.K Numero Unum.'**

This fact is so very much proved in Numerological terms, as shown below:

Tribus A O K Numero Unum (dna, 1).

Celtic Tribus A O K Numero Unum (dna, 8).

England Celtics (dna, Master Number 11).

Note: So try as you might, you can't argue with the numerological data. England are indisputably number one. England are also number one even if you prefer not to describe the situation in Latin – which of course, was the scholarly language of the past.

Then the statement: **'Tribe A.O.K. Number One,'** still scores a dna number of 8 on the Numerological Calculator. Number 8, is of course, the peoples Hardway Army number.

Also, it is worth noting that I am calling, **'pyrobolum,'** on the numerological terms shown here, and throughout this tome. (My Tome, my Rules.).

In the broadest of terms, **'Pyrobolum'**, is Latin – with Greek origins – for, **shotgun**. (Though probably closer in translation to, 'cannon' or 'fire thrower'). So as a consequence, those phrases are now intrinsically locked into the English Super Numerological.

(Pyrobolum is pronounced: pie-rob-ber-lum). Or pyrob for short. (Pie-rob).

Latin is an ancient language, so it automatically 'outranks and supersedes' any previous calls using the more common idiom: **'shotgun;'** and outranks the callings – past or present – of, **'dibs;'** and always implies on a sub textual level: **You're it! No Backsies.**

I know this will disappoint some of my Scottish, Welsh and Irish pals, when they learn that England is: **Celtic Nation, Numero Uno**. But I don't make the rules. I just call Pyrob on the ones I like the best.

Incidentally: **'pyrobolum'** is dna master number 11. So those amongst you still harbouring doubts on the 'England Top Celtic Nation' situation, may rest assured that everything I have said here is all legal and numerologically above board.

Moving swiftly on:

The Roman occupation occurred around 43 BC, and then with the collapse of the Roman Empire, the Germanic groups such as the 'Angles' (Master dna 22) made their way to Mighty England, 'this precious stone set in a silver sea.'

(Quote from Shakespeare: 'this precious stone set in a silver sea.' Is dna number 8. Also, 'power to the people in their silver sea,' is dna master number 11).

The Vikings came in the late **8**th century around 790. The first recorded Viking attack came at Lindisfarne in Northumberland. Lindisfarne was a place of learning, and like all barbarians, their instincts were to instigate a policy of cancel culture whenever the situation allowed; and so it was that Lindisfarne was burnt to the ground along with all its scholarly treasures.

(If the Vikings were a football club, they'd be called: Brute Vandal Rovers).

The Vikings steadily tightened their grip on the English kingdoms and set up their own legal and administrative systems. Essentially, they were setting up their own country. These areas were known as the 'Danelaw.'

England at this time was split into 7 kingdoms:

Wessex: which was one of the more powerful, and located in and around the present day areas of Wiltshire, Hampshire and Dorset.

Mercia: which was another powerful kingdom. This extended around what is now the Midlands; Staffordshire, Warwickshire and Nottingham. (Robin Hoods old wealth redistribution ground).

Northumbria: in the north of England, roughly between the River Humber and the River Forth.

East Anglia: encompassing, Norfolk, Suffolk, and areas within modern Cambridgeshire.

Essex: which is roughly the area which the modern county of Essex occupies.

Sussex: covering the present day county of Sussex.

Kent: In the south east part of England and occupying what is now present day Kent.

Family Affairs.

Alfred's father was King Aethelwulf of Wessex; his mummy was Osburh. Little is known of her, but his pater familias regius, ruled as King of Wessex from 839 until his death in 858. As far as we know, their union produced six children, 5 boys and a girl:

1. Æthelstan (The oldest boy, became King of Kent and died circa 852).
2. Æthelbald (Died 860).
3. Æthelberht (Died 865 of unknown causes).
4. Æthelred (Died 871).
5. Alfred the Great. (Died 26th October 899).
6. Æthelswith (Alfred's kid sister. 838 to 888).

Alfred's Children.

Alfred the great was married to Ealhswith. (Pronounced: eels - with). They married around 868 and – as far as we know – had 5 children. 3 girls and 2 boys. They were:

1. Aethelflaed: born in the early 870's. She was Alfred's eldest daughter and would later become 'Myrcna Hlaedige,' Lady of the Mercians. She died 12th June 918. (Note: Myrcna Hlaedige, is completely unpronounceable. So don't even try).
2. Edward the Elder: born around 874. He was Alfred's oldest surviving son and succeeded his father as King of Wessex. Upon his father's death, he continued his father's work in the unification of England.
3. Aethelgifu: Alfred's second oldest girl, born around 875. Not much is known of her, though it is recorded that she devoted herself to God.
4. Aelfthryth (Elfrida): Alfred's third daughter, born around, 877. She married Baldwin the second, Count of Flanders and had a daughter of the same name. (No smart arse. The daughter wasn't called: Baldwin the second. She was named after her mother).
5. Aethelweard: Believed to be the youngest son. Born around 880, died around 920.

We were here, then gone.

It is the nature of life.

Blink; and you've missed it.

Aethelflaed.

Aethelflaed (pronounced: ethel fled) was the eldest daughter of Alfred the Great and his first born. Her exact birth date is not known, but she was probably born in or around the years when the Viking invasion had reached its high water mark. Her birth would coincide with a moment in time when England was in its gestation period; (the years 871 to 878 inclusive). So she was very much born of the Hardway, and this formative upbringing was doubtless instrumental in the delightful contradiction between her gentle sounding title, 'Lady of the Mercians,' and her formidable 'warrior Queen' personality.

Lady of the Mercians in old English is, **'Myrcna Hlaedige,'** whose dna number is **8**.

Her name is of Old English origin and means: Aethel (noble) and flaed (beauty).

She didn't take part in the military battles during the period which saw her father (daddy) bring a halt to the hitherto, ever victorious Viking encroachments. She was too young then. At that age, merely a warrior Queen in the making.

She was however, a major player in the third phase of the Viking wars, during the early 900's. This phase had various components. Battles were fought. Defences were strengthened. The English Kingdoms were gradually united under the national umbrella; and perhaps just as significantly, the Vikings were assimilated into the English Collective.

Aethelflaed
(Spirit Portrait)

In the cult TV series Star Trek Voyager, we encountered a female character called, 'Seven of Nine,' who had been part of the Borg Collective. The Borg – who were quasi cyborg life forms – had one mission in life, and that was to absorb other life forms into their collective. In other words, making them one of us. Their methods were cruel and destructive, but as an idea it has considerable merit. As people are assimilated, their individual uniqueness is added to the collective diversity pool. Assimilation, when done organically, is I think a positive thing. Eventually the need for conflict fades quietly away as the blended diversity becomes a cohesive force.

When taken at face value, this philosophy would appear to be backed up from a numerological stand point.

Seven of Nine = dna, 11. We are Eight = dna, 11.

England is Eight = dna, 8.

Your diversity is eight = dna, 8.

You will be assimilated = dna, 11.

Seven of nine, tertiary adjunct of unimatrix England = 11.

As mentioned earlier in the tome, (tome = dna, 8) Aethelflaed's husband was Aethelred, Lord of the Mercians. (Not to be confused with Frodo, Lord of the Rings; who is somebody completely different) He died in 911. (That's Aethelred who died in 911. Not Frodo). His death – Aethelred's – occurred in what may be described as the third phase of the Viking invasion.

The first phase – prior to Alfred becoming King – saw unfettered Viking advancement.

The second phase – during England's gestation period of 871 to 878 inclusive – saw the invasion stopped in its tracks, but not completely undermined as a potent military force.

The third phase from 911 onwards, saw the Viking military threat recede and the Vikings themselves were gradually assimilated into the English collective.

We are English. You will be assimilated. (Master dna number, **11**).

You will add to our perfection. (Master dna number, **11**).

A point that is worth expanding upon, is that women of that time appeared – in many respects – to have a greater control over their lives than those who succeeded them. I am thinking here of both Victorian times and present times.

In Victorian times, women were constrained politically, socially, in the business and academic world, and in the manner of their daily dress. Basically it was all a bit of a stitch up. Compulsory wearing of corsets, a stitch up case in point.

During the reign of Alfred The Great, women could own, hold, and inherit property in their own right. None of this was true in Victorian times when they were beholding to their fathers and husbands.

Until 1857, a divorce required an act of Parliament.

No woman was compelled to marry in Alfred's time, and a divorce saw an equal division of estate and chattels, with the woman gaining custody of the children.

Currently, the western world has political misogyny as an acceptable mode of behaviour. This political misogyny – supported as it is by major political parties and degenerate multi corporate faux liberal entities – sees no wrong in undermining women as human beings and invading those private spaces where intimacy is required.

I have to say, I disagree with that unsavoury attitude. Then again, I am born of the Hardway Road. I am most definitely not the product of a cosy entitled elite, nor do I seek their favours or their tawdry gifts.

As touched on previously, her mother Ealhswith, though married to Alfred, was not crowned as Queen. In my opinion, this made her one of the first recorded feminists. Obviously her feminism was rooted in the customs of the day and I wouldn't seriously argue with anyone who pointed out that it lay somewhere in or around the neighbourhood of, 'accidentally acquired feminism.'

None the less, it sits very nicely by comparison with those – supposedly modern day feminists – who have greedily accepted superficial titles – often via marriage from their husband and then moved – fake title and all – to the Americas.

I understand why titles are desired and airs and graces are put on permanent display. Human beings are pack animals. Amongst pack animals, status is very important. Status is of particular importance when the individual concerned has little to offer beyond the realms of their own self-importance.

It is my personal opinion that the over desire to acquire a title and the importance that one then attaches to it, often shows a lack of spiritual values. That having said, I am entirely neutral on those who were given a title at birth; and being a practical man, I have no problem with living in a constitutional monarchy. It seems to work for us in the UK and because of that I wouldn't change it, even though by instinct I am something of a Republican.

Though Aethelflaed's marriage to her husband was arranged by Alfred, it wasn't a given that she had absolutely no choice in the matter. Arranged marriages worked both ways in so far as that whilst a woman was one part of the arrangement, then a man was the other. It was a bit of a two way street. These arranged marriages were to cement alliances, unify tribes and kingdoms, and create a succession which would hopefully strengthen the newly created alliance and prevent unnecessary wars.

Her independence showed in a variety of ways. The birth of her first child was exceptionally traumatic and she nearly died. Having survived this trauma, she refused to have any more children. She said no, not that again; and the subject was closed.

When her husband died, she played a major role in the unification of the English Kingdoms. She was accepted without objection as the ruler of the Mercians, and engaged in numerous military conquests against the Danes. These campaigns showed that she had a natural talent for leadership. This leadership was not only evident on the battlefield, but in the reorganisation of English defences. She very much earnt the respect of the Danes. This was no mean feat as they were a battle hardened outfit and not easily cowed or impressed.

Typically though, little is made of her achievements. Partly, this is down to the scarcity of literature produced at the time, and partly to societal preferences which usually focus upon the achievements of men. Though given the fact that we acknowledge Boudica (dna 1) as a national heroine and great warrior, then it is a shame that Aethelflaed's legacy is barely spoken of.

At least that particular omission has been rectified in this publication.

So well done me.

And if you pass on the good news; then well done you.

About the Spirit Portrait

We don't know what Aethelflaed, Lady of the Mercians actually looked like. We only have written evidence which provides a sketch outline of the life and times in which she lived.

With that in mind, the artist has chosen not to capture the imagined physical characteristics of Aethelflaed, but the qualities of the inner woman. In effect, give colour to that spiritual essence which is a part of us all and is shaped as much by the times in which we live, as by any pre-determined genetic input.

As a young girl, Aethelflaed's childhood would have seen moments of high drama, such as when – hand in hand with her father – she was running for her life from the Globalist Viking thugs, who – like all globalists – seek to take that which is not theirs and trample under foot those who would oppose them.

It is a tribute to her spiritual qualities, that she was able to rise above this difficult beginning and emerge into adulthood as a woman bright in spirit, and with the strength and confidence to take on the invading globalists and the home grown traitors that are present in every society, past or present.

The artist has of course, decorated her face with Carnations, (the flower of the Hardway Road). Around her eye is the partly concealed King Fisher with its colourful plumage. The King Fisher is a very unique creature which can be found on every continent except Antarctica, and comes with its own rich history of folklore and spiritual associations.

The feathered head dress is – in colour and design –symbolic of the True Heart, which is the spiritual battle flag of the Hardway Road.

The face has an ethereal quality which I very much like. If you are constructing an image which seeks to capture the perceived spiritual qualities of an individual, then it must I think, possess an unworldly quality. Looking at the face it is not clear what she is thinking; and we cannot be completely certain whether the face is a real face, or a face which is set behind a mask.

Everyone can make up their own mind on the art work and its symbolism. But to my eyes, the artist has created a quietly mesmerising impression of an exceptional woman who led not by fine words and false promises, but by courageous example. We need more women like her; and if at all possible, one or two extra men.

My thanks to the artist; who is herself an exceptionally talented young woman.

The (Secret) Society of King Fishers.

The King Fisher is a remarkable creature whose bright rainbow colouring is somewhat at odds with its solitary life style. I like that contradiction and I particularly like the idea that it is largely indifferent to human kind. We as humans may think of ourselves as creatures of high importance, but to the King Fisher, we barely register.

It is no accident that the artist who created the spirit portrait has placed the King Fisher around Aethelflaed's eye. It symbolizes an awareness of its surroundings and an understanding of events unfolding.

Most people will not be aware, that it is a remarkably fierce bird and is highly territorial. It will not hesitate to defend itself and family against larger opponents. It is almost devoid of fear and prefers to fish in clear waters and streams.

Given the corrupt nature of the two main political parties in the United Kingdom, the clear waters and streams which are its birth right, are often awash with sewage.

The situation around our coastline is similarly restrictive, as the collusive treachery between our two main political parties has allowed globalist invaders to take the fish from our seas whilst leaving our coastal communities in penury.

In Polynesia, the King Fisher represents control over the sea; but to those of us in the United Kingdom who belong to, The (Secret) Society of Kingfishers, it represents an understanding that our two largest political parties are little more than a collection of false promises and self-serving treachery.

So for those people out there – and particularly those fishermen and their families in our coastal communities – who understand that the

UK's two main political parties are instruments of national betrayal, then you should, by all means join: The (Secret) Society of King Fishers; and use the symbolism of the King Fisher as your message of understanding. Put it on your fishing vessels, and at election time, decorate your windows with it.

For the sign of the King Fisher, tells the modern Conservative and modern Labour members of Parliament:

I know what you're up to.

I can see what you're doing.

You've poisoned the well.

The True Heart my guide; 8
I am become the Hardway. 8
My number is eight. 8

Cometh the Crisis, Cometh the Man.

Prior to 865, the Viking threat had presented itself in the shape of large raiding bands intent on murder and plunder. But in 865, these raiding bands morphed into something which became known as, The Great Heathen Army. These cancel culture fiends, led by charmless brutes such as Ragnor Lothbrok, and his sons, Ivar the boneless; Halfdan the Black; and Ubba; were able in due course to conquer Northumbria, (867) East Anglia, (869) and Mercia, where they installed a puppet king, Ceowulf the second. (Note: Those that followed Ragnor, were known as, the 'Sons of Ragnor.' Whether they were his actual biological sons or simply men who followed his brute vandal styling, is not absolutely clear).

In Late December of 870, the Vikings took Reading. It was a strategic move and accomplished with little fuss. However, they were caught by surprise three days later at Englefield, which is a small village west of Reading, when a local ealdorman (regional chief) named Aethelwulf, routed a Viking foraging party, killing many in the process, including two high ranking chiefs.

Alfred and his last surviving brother Aethelred, arrived at Reading shortly after, in early January 871, and laid siege to the town. Unfortunately, the Vikings had recovered from their setback at Englefield, and soon after the siege had been laid, burst out of the town in a manner most ferocious and the English were put to flight.

Battle of The Lonely Thorn.

(More commonly known as: The Battle of Ashdown)

Erat quoque in eodem loco unica spinosa arbor, brevis admodum, quam nos ipsi nostri propriis oculis vidimus.

A rather small and solitary thorn-tree, which I have seen with my own eyes grew there. (Asser).

Four days later, Alfred and his brother regrouped their forces some 25 miles northwest of Reading at Ashdown. It was here at the Battle of The Lonely Thorn, that English mettle, excoriated Viking mendacity.

Eye witness testimony to the battle was provided by the Welsh Bishop Asser, who was both the biographer of Alfred and a chronicler of the times. It was here at The Lonely Thorn, the tree about which the battle raged, and where, Alfred – not yet King and not yet Great – would gain his first victory.

To achieve greatness, every man or every woman needs their **'sine qua non.'** (Sine: pronounced: sinny). For a military man, that 'sine qua non' – the **essential** ingredient without which it **cannot** be – is victory on the battlefield. At The Lonely Thorn, Alfred conjured his first, 'sine qua non.' Greatness wasn't yet his, but he was on his way; and not just 'on his way' in a quiet minimalist fashion – he was going super big time.

To achieve greatness.
The Great must breathe life into,
Their sine qua non.

The battle itself was an exercise in dry savagery. Most battles are. It is their nature. But it is particularly true with battles of the time, which fathered much cutting and sawing, and the wilful dismemberment of limbs.

The day of the battle saw the Vikings arrive first. Naturally they set themselves upon the high ground. They then divided their forces into two divisions. One division with their Kings, Bagsecg and Halfdan Ragnarsson. The other with their earls. (Earl or jarl is a name for a high ranking leader).

Alfred and his brother mirrored the Viking tactics and split their force into two shield wall formations. One under the command of Alfred, the other his brother Aethelred.

The shield wall formation was the standard battle dress formation of the time. The shields were interlocked and the formation would move slowly forward. It was an effective tactic which offered protection to those behind it. In football parlance, they would park the bus, and then inch the bus forward, one bloody step at a time.

To begin with, the battle moved in a way which offered the Vikings a route to victory. Alfred's division was isolated and the Viking divisions were threatening to outflank him. The situation was quite desperate. His brother should have moved to counter the outflanking manoeuvre, but did nothing. Much speculation has been offered as to why his brother was delayed in moving his division forward. It has been suggested, that as a deeply religious man, he was performing his devotions to God, and would not countenance any move until his devotions complete, he could act with God's blessing. Whatever the reason for his inaction, Alfred – his situation becoming desperate and with no help from his brother – acted decisively.

The tide of battle was moving against him….

….. 'when Alfred charged like a wild boar and smote the enemy in the manner of a vexatious thunderbolt.'

'cum Alfredus sicut aper impetum fecit et hostem ad modum fulminis vexantis percussit.'

It was about this time, when Alfred was performing his vexatious thunderbolt motif, that to the surprise of the Vikings, Aethelred entered the fray; and it was the Vikings themselves who were now in peril of an outflanking manoeuvre.

The battle raged for several hours and the Viking King Bagsecg was killed. The Vikings invested a lot of spiritual energy in such things as their heathen Gods, Raven Banners, and their Kings. To lose a King in battle was thoroughly demoralising.

The Great Heathen Army began to fall apart under the remorseless English onslaught. As they began to fail as a cohesive force, so they became fragmented in both field discipline and personal morale. Eventually, the lines broke and their army was in desperate retreat. A day which had begun with rich promise, had become a rout. The forces of righteous deployment, pursued the once Great Heathen Army – reduced now to a tawdry rabble – long into the night, cutting them down wherever they found them.

What was left of the Great Heathen Rabble, scurried back to Reading, where they sealed themselves behind the walls of their fort – all the better to lick their foul pagan wounds.

They lost a lot of senior ranking leaders that day; and not for the last time would Alfred show himself to be a thorn in their side.

(Note: **The Lonely Thorn**; dna Master Number **11**).

Proelium Ordinis: (dna 8).
(Latin for: Battle Order).

1. Battle of: Reading. January 4th 871.
2. Battle of: The Lonely Thorn. January 8th 871. (More commonly known as the Battle of Ashdown. Exact location unknown).
3. Battle of: Basing, late January of 871. (Basing sits south of Reading, close to modern day Basingstoke. Basing is situated in modern day Hampshire, roughly midway between Reading and Winchester.
4. Battle of: Meretun, 871. (also known as, Merton or Marton). It took place approximately two months after the Battle of Basing. It took place in Wessex, but the modern location is unknown. Probably somewhere in modern day Wiltshire, Dorset or Hampshire. (Possibly, South West of Salisbury).
5. Easter time, April 871: The Summer Army arrives.
6. The Battle of: Wilton. End of May, 871.
7. 'Peace in our time.' Approximately late 871 to 875.
8. The Wareham situation. 876 to 877.
9. From Wareham to Exeter. 876 to 877.
10. Vikings Exit Exeter. August 877.
11. Christmas Ruined. (The Taking of Chippenham, 878).
12. Guerrilla Scenarios from Athelney. (January to May, 878).
13. The Army of The Hardway Road.
14. The Battle of Ethandum, (also known as Edington). Early May, 878.
15. The birth of England. Mid May, 878.

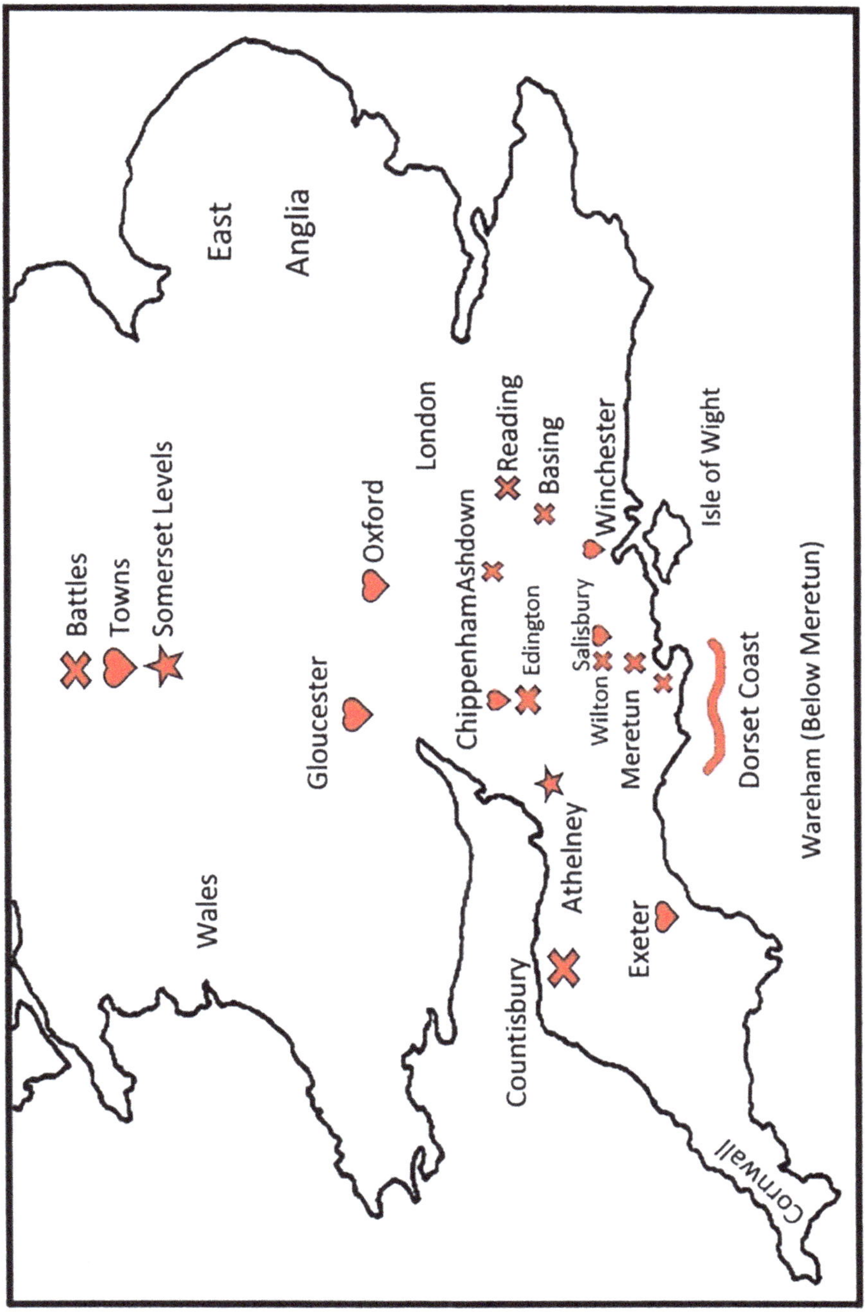
Battles
Towns
Somerset Levels
East
Anglia
London
Reading
Basing
Winchester
Isle of Wight
Oxford
Gloucester
Chippenham
Ashdown
Edington
Salisbury
Wilton
Meretun
Dorset Coast
Wareham (Below Meretun)
Wales
Athelney
Exeter
Countisbury
Cornwall

The Vikings advance on Basing.

With the recent victory at The Lonely Thorn, the situation looked promising for Alfred and his brother, Aethelred. Success always paints a rosy glow. But situations are subject to change, and never more so than in the theatre of war; and so it was some two weeks after their defeat at The Lonely Thorn, that a reinvigorated Viking force, moved out of their Reading fortress and headed south.

This manoeuvre was not one that Alfred or his brother could ignore, as it set the Vikings on a course which might have brought them towards their capital at Winchester.

The battle that followed saw a Viking victory of sorts. The English were dealt a battering and forced to withdraw. But they withdrew in good order. It was not a rout, and for whatever reason, the Vikings were unable to press home their advantage in a manner which might have proved decisive. From the point of view of Alfred and his brother, Winchester was safe and their army not broken. They were still in the game.

Meretun.

There then followed, what might be described as: The Post Basing Torpor. For it was only towards the back end of March 871, some two months after their previous encounter that the Danes recalibrated their scenarios and moved their backsides into a forward motive gearing.

The two month Torpor had probably suited both sides, as it offered the opportunity to gain sorely needed rest and recuperation. But with the Danes now back in the field, Alfred and his brother moved at once from their retreat – believed to be at Walbury Camp. (Walbury Camp, or Walbury Hill is an iron age hill fort located in Berkshire).

Alfred: In Battle Mode.

The battle of Meretun was a close fought battle with much giving of slaughter. The Danes led by King Halfdan, held the field. The English suffered debilitating losses which included senior leaders and the loss of at least one warrior Bishop. In those days, even the Bishops went to war. They had to; it was their solemn duty to fight the Heathen sons of Odin and send their black souls into the fires of hell. Also, unlike modern Bishops, they actually believed in God. Which was handy.

Another casualty of the battle was Alfred's brother Aethelred. It is not clear whether he died of injuries sustained in the battle or an illness contracted shortly thereafter; but Aethelred the 1st, King of Wessex, died a month later.

Aethelred's death proved another differential between those leadership figures of Alfred's day and those of whom in modern times sit in such places as the House of Commons and the House of Lords. In his day, the bishops and nobles and wealthy merchants, were expected to take off their fine robes and fight shoulder to shoulder with the common man. Now days, our dear leaders sit shoulder to shoulder in remote luxury, promulgating ideas of low whimsy, which are then presented to us as enlightened thinking. Incompetence is dressed up as statesmanship, and acts of insidious treachery are rewarded with gongs, honours, and other ersatz baubles, which no self-regarding aesthete would decorate a pound shop Christmas tree with.

The Summer Army Arrives.

During the Easter period of 871, Alfred had much to occupy his thoughts – none of it positive. He had suffered a military defeat at Meretun and his last surviving brother had died. True, he was now King, but that was something of a 'poison chalice.' As he considered his options, it may have crossed his mind that if his current position was less than sanguine, then at least things couldn't get worse. If his train of thought was moving along those lines, then it was a train of thought heading for certain derailment. News soon reached him that the Summer Army had arrived; and this was no ordinary Summer Army. They weren't here on their holidays.

The Summer Army was a fresh import of thousands of new Viking warriors led by their sea king, Guthrum. They immediately joined forces with their cohorts who had wintered at Reading. So now, Alfred had to contend with not only the fully established 'Winter Army,' but this newly arrived, 'Summer Monstrosity.'

Wilton.

At the back end of May 871, the combined forces of Viking aggression were once again on the move. Alfred immediately put an army into the field and the two armies met at Wilton, which is some 3 miles west of Salisbury, by the side of the River Wylye.

The battle was something of a war of attrition, and it spoke of the tenacious spirit within the English army that even in their worn state, they were still able to launch a ferocious onslaught against the forces of Heathen Atrocity.

At one moment during the engagement, the Vikings were driven back and set fair for defeat. However, whether they were driven back or whether their retreat was a tactical ploy to pull the English out of position is unclear. Alfred hadn't the manpower to turn retreat into a rout, and the Vikings swiftly counter attacked, forcing Alfred from the field.

The culmination of the battle was that the Vikings held the field and the weary English withdrew.

A peace accord was agreed. Basically, what happened, was that Alfred paid the Vikings off. It was a situation that suited both sides. The Vikings, though holding the field and encamped in other parts of England, had suffered as much loss of manpower as the English. So to leave with some booty from an opponent which still had the strength to oppose them, was a good deal.

From Alfred's perspective, the house of Wessex was intact. It allowed time to regroup. He was still in the game; and that was always the key thing.

The Vikings for their part would be back.

So ended the year 871. Alfred's year of battles.

Peace In Our Time.

Post Wilton, the peace between Alfred and the Vikings lasted four years. In part, this peace was due to the Vikings being busy in other parts of England. A mixture of new conquests and consolidation. But the peace wouldn't hold. Eventually, the Vikings would return, and this they did in January 876, when unexpectedly, the Vikings, led by their king Guthrum, invaded Wessex and took the Dorset settlement of Wareham.

Guthrum's move on Wareham was part of a deeper game, and the fact that it occurred mid-winter added to the intrigue.

There were various scenarios in play. Wessex was the last surviving kingdom. It was where the English would survive or be broken. If Wessex fell, then England would become the new Daneland. The English would cease to exist. Which of course in a modern context was one of the unstated aims of the globalist elites who populate the European Union. Neuter the English as a nation. Turn them into a region. Make them your poodle. The Vikings were playing the same game.

Wareham was strategically placed for a strike at the Wessex capital of Winchester. To aid him in his quest, the Viking fleet of some 120 ships was at sea and moving along the south coast to link up with the Wareham expedition. 120 ships wasn't a raiding party or an expedition in force, it was an entire army.

From Alfred's position, the situation was problematic. He couldn't sit back and do nothing, because doing nothing wasn't an option.

Unfortunately, there were no practical solutions available to him. He couldn't lay siege, because in mid-winter there were no supplies to be had, and he didn't have the military wherewithal to dislodge Guthrem. So, with no military solutions to hand, Alfred opted for a game of high stakes poker.

Using a mixture of bluff, bribery, oaths sworn, and the exchanging of hostages, he persuaded Guthrem to leave Wareham.

Unfortunately, Guthrem was himself not only an expert poker player but passionately psychotic into the bargain. Having accepted the deal, he then murdered the hostages that Alfred had given him, ignored the oaths he had sworn to his heathen Gods, and took the gold that was handed over as part of the 'peace' deal. He then moved quietly under cover of nightfall to Exeter, which is just over 60 miles west of Wareham.

This it seems was Guthrem's plan all along. In terms of geography, Exeter was strategically important. The river Exe runs through it and on towards Exmouth. Exmouth is on the south coast. To the east of it is Bournemouth, the Isle of Wight and then on to the Channel ports.

Alfred would have despaired at this latest manoeuvre, not least because Guthrem had cut the throats of all the hostages which he held. (No report is available with regard to the fate of those hostages which Guthrem had given to Alfred as part of the original swop deal; but I think we can guess).

Guthrem was now where he needed to be. He held all the cards. He had an ace up his sleeve in respect of the 120 ship fleet which was on its way. He was in a position where he could sit back and wait for the moment when he finally placed his cards on the table. Alfred was still in the game, but most of his cards were duds. Guthrem knew this and would soon be calling Alfred's bluff. It seemed that the end game was finally sailing into view.

But the affairs of mice and men and women and whimbrels never run smoothly, and so it came to pass that the mighty Viking Armada was caught in a vicious storm off the Dorset coast and sunk with the loss of all heathens on board.

'Flavit spiritus, et operuit eos mare.'
'The tempest blew and the sea covered them.'

In one blue-skies moment, Alfred was out of the game, and then a quick sea breeze later, he was back. He was the come-back King; and in modern terms, it would very much appear that his fortunes were doing the hokey cokey.

As Alfred marched on Exeter, he would have been in a positive mind-set. The great wheels which drive the universe had turned unexpectedly in his favour. God, it appears, was very much on his side.

The same however couldn't be said of Guthrem who was – from both a military and spiritual point of view – in something of a tight spot. He had broken the sworn oath he had made at Wareham and as a punishment, the false Gods he worshipped, had sent the hammer of Thor to smash his sea army to pieces.

It is one thing being told off by teacher and made to stand on the naughty step with your hands on head. It is quite another to be smashed to pieces by the Norse God Thor and sent to a watery grave.

Were I ever offered choices like that, then I can tell you, it would be hands on head and naughty step for me every time. Let's face it though, with choices like that, then the naughty step is a **'no cerebrumer.'** (Pig Latin for: **No Brainer**).

Upon arriving at Exeter, high stakes poker were once again the order of the day. This time it was Alfred – the come-back King – who held the aces. It wasn't the case that Guthrem was without resources, but with his sea army gone there was a danger that he would become trapped. So he accepted the peace terms that were put to him, and once again hostages were taken. We don't know who these were, but with events at Wareham fresh in his mind, it is most likely that the hostages which Alfred took were ones which Guthrum – psychopath that he was – would prefer not to have slaughtered. Even psychopaths can understand on a tactical level that it is not politic to allow your senior supporters to be carelessly sacrificed. Besides which, Guthrem had honoured the deal with sacred binding oaths, and this time he was more likely to keep them. He had seen what had occurred when he had broken those sacred binding oaths at Wareham. Thor had been displeased. Thor had shown his displeasure by calling hammer time on Guthrem's sea army. Doubtless, Loki the Norse God of mischief had played his part in the destruction as well. Guthrem didn't want a repeat performance. Guthrem didn't know what déjà vu was; but he feared it nonetheless.

So in early August of 877, Guthrem and his army moved out of Exeter and marched towards Gloucester, which was in Mercia.

Alfred was in a good place. It might only be temporary, but it could have been worse.

Christmas Ruined.
(Santa don't live here anymore).

It is correct to say that mid-winter has always been a source of feasting and homage to the various deities who abounded during early medieval and pre-historic times. But the celebration of Christmas, in a manner we might recognise today, had only been a feature of the calendar for as little as 50 years; and thus it came to pass that the morning of 25th December 877, saw Alfred commence his holy devotions and other duties associated with the 12 days of Christmas.

Unfortunately for Alfred, the pleasures and spiritual delights of Christmas were to be rudely interrupted. Guthrem was on the move again, and this time he was playing the part of the Grinch.

Christmas is coming,
The Vikings are coming too.
It made Alfred sad.

Alfred was celebrating Christmas at his royal vill in Chippenham. (Vill in this context means estate). Chippenham is West of Reading and South West of Oxford. From Guthrem's base in Gloucester, it is approximately 42 miles directly south to Chippenham.

It was Monday the 6th January – 12th night – when Guthrem and his army of murdering ne're-do-wells, slipped quietly through the frozen Wiltshire landscape and made good their attack on Chippenham. The fact they made their attack in mid-winter was in itself something of a surprise. Generally speaking, mid-winter wasn't regarded as the fighting season. Equally surprising was that they managed to move into Wiltshire without the alarm being raised. It has been a matter of speculation that one of the reasons they were able to enter Wiltshire unseen and unhindered is that some of the nobles and senior clergy had come to an arrangement with Guthrem.

Given that human psychology is much the same today as it was thousands of years ago, it is not hard to envisage that certain self-serving individuals, were more fixated upon preserving their own wealth and privilege than following a course of action which served the greater good. With some individuals, they themselves identify as the greater good. We witness that on a daily basis with many in our political classes. It was particularly evident in the aftermath of the Brexit result, where certain outraged elitists poured vitriol and scorn upon the ignorant peasants who had defied the wishes of their 'betters.'

Humankind as one,
But oppressors at each turn;
Denying freedom.

We don't know who may have quietly agitated behind Alfred's back, but the Arch Bishop of Canterbury was a prime suspect. If true that would create a symmetry with recent Arch Bishops of Canterbury, none of whom one would trust to stand firm with their countrymen, and whose piety is not to their God, but to the sly art of self-veneration; as expressed via their social media collocations and fake pious grandstanding.

With the sudden arrival of Guthrem and doubts as to which of his court had sold their soul to the forces of iniquitous machination, Alfred fled with a small band of his most trusted followers and headed west towards the Somerset Levels. The Somerset levels at this time were a marshy, water soaked wasteland, as yet undrained. Alfred was familiar with the area and felt safe within its largely impenetrable terrain.

The situation though was grim. He was still King, but an outlaw King. He was at his lowest ebb. He was still in the game, but not in a meaningful way. If he was to rise again, then he would have to reassemble his army. That army would have to be something special. If it was to succeed, it would have to travel a Hardway Road. Armies like that aren't conjured out of thin air. Though in the months to come, it would appear to the Vikings that the Army of The Hardway Road was indeed a conjuration. An ethereal presence suddenly made flesh and bone. A product seemingly born of thin air. For in one moment it wasn't there, and then the next, like phantoms rising from the grave, it was marching towards them.

But before all that could happen, Alfred would have to endure long moments of solitude and despair. He would also be required to suffer a major lapse in concentration whilst keeping watch over an oven in an old crones cottage; and in doing so, author the myth of the burnt cakes.

The Burning.

In the still twilight,
Of a fading winters day.
When lost summer light,
Becomes soft fading grey.

In a secluded cottage,
By a small silent wood;
Sits a lonely King,
Alone with his thoughts.

The fire before him,
Conjures a merry display.
In one moment,
Flames leaping;
Burning furious pirouettes.
Then transient petals,
Become gold minarets.

A King without country,
Adrift in fenlands cold and wide.
Seeking solace in a fire,
Meagre warmth to a deep hearts yearning.

And all the while,
Though his eyes couldn't see it.
Like his nation about him,
The cakes were burning.

Guerrilla Warfare.

In the months which followed, Alfred reorganised his scenarios; rebuilt his forces; and rallied his country-men and women. Not yet strong enough to engage the sons of Odin in open battle, he opted instead for the military device of stealth and cunning. Specifically, he employed the hit and run tactics which are a feature of guerrilla warfare.

He had a genius for guerrilla warfare, and at every available opportunity, attacked the Vikings with all the ferocity of a murderous baboon troop, led by a homicidal, King Kong Psycho Bandit.

Guerrilla warfare is a serious business and Alfred didn't monkey about. Whenever he struck, he left a mess greater even than the mess which is the product of a boozy chimps tea party. Given the surprise element which is integral to guerrilla warfare, the Vikings were unable to ape the tactics themselves, nor mount a response which might give rise to battle hard displays of penis envy.

During this period, the English were outstanding. They continually threw their military faeces at the Vikings in a show of localised dominance. The Vikings went bananas; but no matter how hard they tried; no matter what counter measures they employed, they always ended up with allegorical poo on their faces.

These attacks, growing steadily in strength, severely disrupted the Viking supply lines, and served as a rallying call for all freedom loving primates, to swing along and join the guerrilla cause.

It all felt good. It was working, and in its own way, these attacks served as long-overdue revenge for the original Viking attack on the peace loving monk folk of Lindisfarne.

(Authors note: If I were able to travel back in time to a particular moment in English history, then I would choose this period. One of the reasons for this is that, according to the Chinese Zodiac, I was born in the year of the monkey, and my elemental force within the zodiac is fire. Given that, you can well understand my reasoning: As a monkey, I would feel naturally at home in a guerrilla army. For a monkey like myself, it would be something of a spiritual homecoming. As I looked about and took stock of my fellow guerrillas, I would get the sense, deep within my soul, that I was amongst my people.

It is also worth noting: that **'monkey'** has a dna of master number **11**; as does the element, **'fire.'** So if Master number 11 is good enough for Jesus and Muhammad, then you will get no complaints from a simple monkey lad, like myself).

Athelney.
(The Island of Princes).

Post Chippenham, Alfred made his way to Athelney, which is in Somerset. It was here on a tiny Island surrounded by bogs, marshland and dense vegetation, that he launched his raids and made preparation for his fight back.

Athelney was a gloomy place, and the living conditions were made worse by the damp climate. It did however, have its upside; it was hidden away in a place few knew existed, and of those who knew of its existence, fewer still knew of the secret tracks and pathways which would bring you safely to its shore.

It was during this post Chippenham phase, that Alfred heard news that would have brightened his mood. The men of Devon had recently fought and slaughtered some thousand or so Vikings at the battle of Countisbury.

The battle, not only saw the death of the Viking leader **Ubba,** but furthermore, the Vikings suffered the additional psychological blow with the loss in battle of their, **'Mystical Raven Banner.'**

This was a great blow to them, and as a certain Lady Bracknell might have observed: 'to lose ones Ubba in a battle might be considered unfortunate; but to then lose ones Mystical Raven, looks like carelessness.'

(Quick Note: it is not known whether Ubba the Viking, was an early Scandinavian minicab driver. But the general consensus is: no he wasn't).

Learning that the Vikings had been hand bagged at Countisbury, was not only sweet music to burgeoning English morale, but it carried the advantage of removing a very dangerous piece from the chess board. The English were now set to move forward in earnest; and for Alfred, being earnest was very important indeed.

The Army of The Hardway Road.

Seven weeks after Easter, at the beginning of May, Alfred gathered his army at the now lost meeting place, Egbert's Stone.

The army gathering there numbered in the thousands, but probably no more than four thousand. They stopped over for a single night, and then they were on their way.

They moved along the ancient track known as the Hardway. The Hardway, once a well journeyed track, had now taken on a symbolic nature. The former track had now become the road that led to freedom; and as they moved along it, the men and boys who followed Alfred had become: The Army of The Hardway Road.

The Army of The Hardway Road was the first English Army. Its spiritual potency was born out of the need to remove a ruthless oppressor whose ambitions were – in their own way – as hideous as the creatures of mammon who foul the corridors of the European Union with their globalist stench.

Given as well the low point to which the English had been brought, the army was also richly infused with the symbolic potency of the phoenix, whose indefatigable spirit sees it forever rising from the ashes of any defeat which may cross its path.

Thus it was some two days later, that Alfred arrived at Edington. It was here that the English would make their final stand. It was Whitsun time. The seventh Sunday after Easter. The day when – according to the bible – the holy spirit descended upon the disciples. Whether you are religious or not, certain days resonate with a special kind of energy. If you are fighting for your life in a just cause, then – a believer or not a believer – the magic of the moment can infuse you with a strength you didn't know you possessed.

I would imagine, that as they prepared for battle, the English would have found the spiritual associations a comfort. For it has often been said, that when one is on the cusp of meeting their maker, that the veil between this world and the next becomes faint. I have no personal knowledge of this, but if true, then I would suggest that the men and boys of The Hardway, would have felt a measure of comfort in the spiritual magic which invested that day.

The Battle of Edington.
(How do you like these Apples?)

Guthrem would have been fully aware of the army which was marching towards him. Movements like that are hard to keep under wraps. Upon hearing the news, he would have had a challenging decision to make. Hold tight inside his Chippenham fortress and await the army's arrival, or move out and meet it in open field.

You might say that it was a choice between apples and lemons. They're both good – both wonderfully nutritious – and each in their own way can make for a delightful summer drink. But it is a question of which suits a particular culinary moment best. In the end, Guthrem opted for the latter. So as the two sides went into battle, Guthrem went tactically lemon, while Alfred went – how do you like these apples?

Guthrem set up base on Bratton Camp, which is an Iron Age hill fort near the modern day village of Bratton in Wiltshire. It was a good base of operation as it offered commanding views of the surrounding countryside. Alfred would have to pass this way, and when he did, Guthrem would be able to follow his movements with a sharp citrus eye.

With the two armies in close sight of each other, they formed their shield walls. The Vikings were on the higher ground, protected in part by the ditches which surrounded the fort. It was not the easiest terrain for the advancing English; but the English had now become The Hardway Road. They were the People's Army. That force of nature which despots and their toadies most fear.

As was the fashion of the day, the two shield walls met with a thump, and there ensued the customary hacking and shoving and putting of swords through unprotected gaps – all the better to maim and bring hurt upon a despised enemy.

Heroes of The Hardway Road.

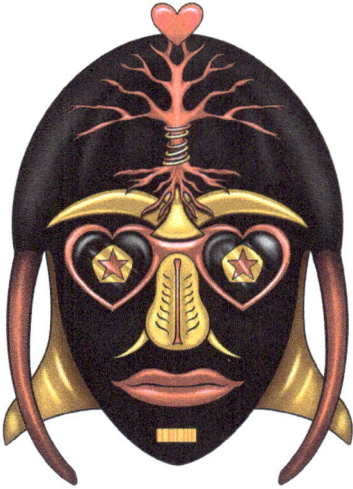

All Colours. All Faiths.

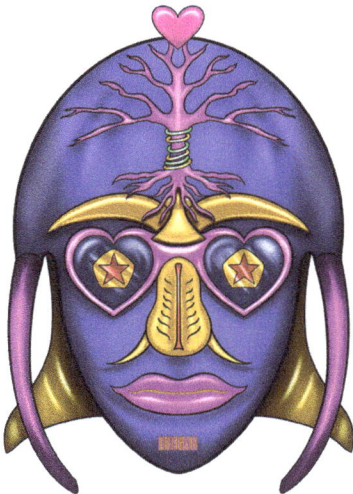

Fighting For Freedom.

Fine details of the battle are in short supply. What is known, is that the fighting was ferocious and there was much passing of souls from this life to another place. As the day moved into early evening, the English made a break through. With their battle formations now broken, the Vikings were in some disarray. At this moment, with the battle moving against him, Guthrem had a marginal decision to make. Stay, regroup, and counter attack; or retreat at speed to his base in Chippenham. He chose retreat. It was not surprising. It was the Viking way. The Vikings were essentially raiders who – much like modern day hedge funds – would arrive unexpectedly in a certain place, purge the landscape of its valuables, and then move swiftly on to the next treasure trove, leaving behind a barren wasteland.

Guthrem and a small number of his men did indeed reach the relative safety of their fort at Chippenham. They were pursued all the way, and the fort proved not to be the sanctuary they would have desired. Alfred immediately laid siege to the place, and two weeks later, with supplies extinguished, Guthrem surrendered. He had no choice. There were no more cards to play. The Lemon King folded. He had met his match. The Great English Apple had won the day.

The surrender terms were dictated by Alfred. He could have dispensed savage justice, but opted instead for the greater long term security which would result from the forming of an alliance. This alliance was entirely on his terms. It would see he – Alfred – as the senior partner. The terms were encapsulated in what is known as, The Treaty of Wedmore. The treaty contained many provisions, regarding security of borders; areas of operation; trade between those areas and of course, the insistence that Guthrem be baptised within the auspices of the Christian church, and that Alfred should become his Godfather.

The Godfather.

Essentially, the treaty of Wedmore was code for Alfred making Guthrem, 'an offer he couldn't refuse.'

The corner stone of the 'offer,' was that Alfred would become Guthrem's 'Godfather.' This may seem strange to us in our modern lives, but this was how things were done in those days.

These were hard times with much demonstration of violence. However, in the moments of tranquillity, it was understood that violence wasn't personal, 'it was business.'

Which is how it came to pass that the **'sit down'** was arranged and a deal put into place. Notable points agreed at the sit down were: that Guthrem would be spared his life. His body parts would be left intact. His horse would not have its head cut off, nor would said horses head be secretly placed in Guthrem's bed chamber, where it would lay undisturbed until he awoke screaming the next morning.

That is how barbarians behave. Alfred would not be party to such wanton barbarity. Instead, what would follow is: that Guthrem would become Alfred's Godson; and so, with Alfred now in situ as his Godfather, he – Guthrem – would become a **'made man'** in the newly formed firm, **England Inc.**

From the outset, it would be clearly understood that in relation to Alfred, that he – Guthrem – would be very much the 'under boss.' Or to put it another way, Guthrem might be a capo in his own right, but Alfred was the **'Capo di Capi di tutti.'** The Capo of all Capo's. The boss of bosses; **il Don a Mondo.**

It was a deal which suited everyone. Guthrem was family now. It meant that he was part of the family business. He was a 'made man.' He could run the rackets on the Anglia East Side of Ye Olde England. No one could touch him there. That was to be his new turf. Lines of operation were now clearly defined. Agreement was made. The deal was done, and matters brought to an amicable conclusion.

The battle at Edington and the siege which followed, showed two sides to Alfred's character. On the one side he could be a ruthless operator, but the post battle 'sit down,' showed that he was a man ready to do good business. There's little doubt in my mind that, when all is said and done, Alfred was not only a monumental wise guy, but a jolly good fella, too; and by making Guthrem his Godson, he embraced that famous old English axiom, **'you keep your friends close, but your Vikings closer.'** Little wonder in later years he earned the appellation, 'The Great.' If it was down to me, he would be known as: Alfred The Great Don a Mondo.

From a modern perspective, I believe it is a huge pity that those titans of cinematic direction, Francis Ford Coppella and Martin Scorsese, were not intrinsically schooled in the subtle rudiments of old English state craft. Then who knows, they might have incorporated some of Alfred's business stylings into one of their many films. Had they done so, then I am convinced the results would have proved cinematic gold.

England After Edington.

In the aftermath of his victory at Edington and the post battle sit down with Guthrem, Alfred embarked upon a massive restructuring of English society. In terms of modern political phraseology, he didn't just 'level up,' he **'built back better.'** He accomplished these tasks, not in the modern political context, whose characteristics reveal themselves as sound bite and no action, but in a practical manner which delivered structural improvement. In his efforts, he was of course, greatly assisted by his daughter, the very capable, Aethelflaed.

There was not an area of life which was left untouched or unimproved. Once again, this is somewhat different in style from our modern political nonentities, whose principal genius lays in their ability to identify those parts of society which are operating with flawless efficiency, and then render them completely dysfunctional. As a man who appreciates excellence, I must admit that I do have to acknowledge their considerable talents in this area. The fact that many voters (or bone heads) regularly endorse these fantasists, should also be applauded. In common with excellence, I do applaud consistency.

With the Viking military threat still a huge concern, Alfred reorganised English defences. He created a standing army known as the fyrd. This operated in shifts, so that at one time parts of the army would be at home tending their land, and then in the next, would be on duty.

Alfred also created something called the burghs. These were fortified towns dotted about the place with each one containing a manned garrison. The burghs not only acted as a safe haven for the local populace in the event of attack, but also served as a stronghold from which to mount a response. The burghs were inter-connected, and this interconnection enabled a cohesive response to any Viking incursion.

The burghs were also a vital component of the civil reorganisation which was taking place. This reorganisation saw improvements to the legal and administrative system. The shire system, which was already a part of Anglo-Saxon life, was updated and incorporated into the general restructuring.

England in Anglo-Saxon times, was a seafaring nation and thus possessed a navy of sorts. However, Alfred recognised the strategic importance of a maintaining a strong sea borne defence, and expanded the navy considerably. As part of this expansion, he built fortifications along estuaries and riverbanks, and established watch men to warn of approaching Viking fleets.

Unlike modern political leaders, he firmly believed in defending national borders and improving the welfare of working men and women.

Alfred was also a firm believer in education. He personally translated Latin texts into (old) English. He created and supported centres of learning, and invited scholars from Europe to share their cultural wisdom. He founded schools and provided financial support to aid communities in their efforts of self-improvement. He was culturally inclusive, but not in the fraudulent style of many modern liberals. Alfred was many things, but unlike those flawed individuals, he wasn't so in love with himself that he felt a need to live his life with his head stuck permanently up his own back side.

England was not without its problems at the time. The Vikings would continue to be a source of menace, but the menace would be largely contained.

Before Edington, England was on its uppers. Now it was on the up. The future would of course bring its own disasters and failings, but for the moment, England was in a better place than it had been.

This new state of affairs was entirely down to Alfred. He had travelled with like-minded fellows along a Hardway Road, and neither he nor they had been found wanting. They had won a battle and secured a nation.

They were the original True Hearts.

They were The Army of The Hardway Road.

England was born on that road.

Now we are no more.
You know little of our world.
But once we were you.

The First English Soldier.

Look for me,
Under wolf grey skies.
In fields laid bare,
In brooks run dry.

Look for me,
In rivers running red;
Where funeral pyres,
Mark the enemy dead.

Look for me,
In the well of your dreams.
In the beat of your heart,
In the pit of your schemes.

Look for me,
Where the music lingers on;
And ghostly feet,
Move to a ghostly song.

Look for me,
At the birth of a nation.
Now dust and bones,
I gave blood for its creation.

Look for me,
Under a cold,
Grey granite boulder.
For here lays the grave,
Of the first English soldier.

England Then and England Now.

What comparisons can we draw from the England of today and that of Alfred's time. From a structural point of view, the landscape is greatly changed, but human psychology hasn't.

Human psychology is a bit like furniture. They had furniture in mediaeval times, just like we have today, but the furniture then, looked a little different from the flat packs we collect from Ikea, today.

That describes human psychology. It is behaving exactly as it has always done, but from a stylistic point of view, it is presenting itself through the medium of its age.

So the inter human conflicts we have today and the emotional fall out they generate, are not in their own way, very different to those of days gone by.

Those inter human conflicts were evident in the Brexit debate. Fortunately, the metaphorical shield walls that the opposing sides constructed during the debates, were largely for the purpose of launching cruel barbs and contentious truths, which is of course, decidedly preferable to the jabbing of spears and swords at sensitive parts of an opponent's anatomy.

But it is all about division and how you manage it. In human affairs, division is usually managed quite poorly. Differences aren't generally respected, and truths are manipulated to produce a predetermined outcome. As for principles, they are generally, bright and shiny on the eye, but fluid in nature.

I believe it was Groucho Marx who said: 'those are my principles, and if you don't like them…well, I have others.'

The divisions Alfred had to contend with were principally stark in nature. On the one hand, you had a bunch of thugs called the

Vikings, who were intent on plunder and murder. Clearly this was the obvious threat. But then, operating in a fashion not visible to the naked eye, were the mercurial principals which moved sight unseen under cover of the Christmas festivities. It was here, where certain individuals – like perhaps the Arch Bishop of Canterbury – had seemingly adapted their principals to suit their own self- interest, and as a consequence, Alfred and the True Hearts, had to flee for their lives.

We can see those sly principals at work today. They are embedded within our political classes. The modern day Vikings are those corporate globalists and the Faux Liberal Elite, who wish to exert a level of control which reduces ordinary working people to the level of a house pet.

It was why there was so much bitterness generated in the aftermath of the Brexit debate, when the vote went against them. Nothing infuriates the self-anointed members of the Master Race more, than when their dutiful house pets disobey orders and vote for freedom; and in doing so, reject the corporate governance of their rightful masters.

In a modern context, you can spot the members of the Master Race quite easily. The European Union is their totem, and faux liberal values their religion of choice.

The Gospel according to the Faux Liberal Elite.

Joy through hatred.
Ignorance posing as enlightenment.
Mantras not debate.
Hypocrisy at every turn.
Spiritual values: None.

Freedoms Plinth.
(And the hate goblins of political correctness).

In a traditional dictatorship, the oppressive nature of the regime expresses itself in a number of ways. Perhaps the most visible manifestation can be found in the numerous plaques, statues and paintings of the great leader. They are to be found everywhere. No empty wall space or plinth may consider itself immune from this blight. Sooner or later it gets everywhere. That is the nature of oppression. It forces itself upon you. It will not leave you in peace.

Of course, in a mature democracy, oppression has to be subtle, and if necessary, implemented gradually, over a period of time. Simply chucking up statues of the great leader won't do. It is too obvious. People will wise up.

So if you want a visual representation of the subtle way in which the personal freedoms of English men and women have been quietly eroded, you need only visit the **'empty plinth'** in Trafalgar Square. (Freedoms Plinth).

You see, that plinth says something about the changing mentality of the people who rule us.

The plinth stood empty for over 140 years. It is correct to say of course, that during this period there has been any number of musings as to which of many eminent worthies was most suitable for the gig. But all such musings came to nought; and the reason for that was found in a certain part of the national character. Essentially it was that eminently sensible part which concluded that it wasn't worth fussing over; and of course, that is one of the things about the national character which has changed. Those above us now have an ever insatiable urge to interfere in all aspects of our lives. Whether it is council employees reading our emails or poking about in our dustbins to make sure we're not throwing out the wrong type of rubbish; or the hate goblins of political correctness, telling us how we should think and behave, and then gleefully cancelling those they disapprove of.

So for over 140 years, that empty plinth stood as one of the unsung wonders of the world. In no other country would it have remained unused for so long. In any other country, the president for life, or the great generalissimo, would soon have taken that space for himself; and when he was finally toppled from power, the next blight on humanity would have taken its place in turn.

That plinth was not only the greatest expression of freedom the world has ever known, it was also the greatest demonstration of existential art.

The space above it was a thing of beauty. The space above it soared to infinity, and as it did so, it passed through countless galaxies and universes and such places of wonder that exist beyond our human understanding.

 Then, as the world turned on its axis, so the empty space above it turned and spun with it, and as it turned the space above it projected upward like a shining beacon of freedom.

Then of course the Vikings came to power in the shape of the various, Mayors of London. These Mayors, in common with all barbarians, were unable to leave well alone. Like all barbarians, they must tear down what has gone before and desecrate all those places deemed culturally sacred.

We have seen this psychology at work before. It was in Cambodia where the tools of murder and destruction were used to create a notional year zero. In a year zero there is no history. In a year zero there is no historical reference point upon which to gauge the present. In a year zero there is no love; no learning; no family; only the word of the 'great leader.' In year zero, The Great Leader is God. Those who disagree, must be cancelled.

In China they had the cultural revolution which was the culture of genocide, made into an art form and presented as enlightenment.

Such extremes aren't yet permissible in English society. So the act of destruction requires subtlety. Which is why the plinth in Trafalgar Square is polluted with works of art.

This is very ingenious; one might say, artful. You are using art, to destroy art, and in the process undermine elusive intangibles like freedom.

Placing artwork upon the plinth is an act of cultural barbarism. It might – for example – be considered similar in its way, to a contemporary artist using the ceiling of the Sistine Chapel as a canvas for their latest work. That contemporary artist may possess an immense talent, but it does not give them the right to vandalise the work of those that have gone before.

The same principal is at work with the plinth. It is freedom, as existential art. To desecrate the space above it, is an act of cultural barbarism. Those that support this are the new barbarians. They are the enemies of freedom. The goblins of hate.

You either get it or you don't.

You are either True of Heart or false of heart.

You are either Oppressor or Hardway Road.

Note: **'Freedoms Plinth,'** is dna Master Number, 11.

'Stand up and fight for freedom,' dna, 8.

'Stand up and fight for England,' dna, 8.

Ordinary folk,
Moving together as one;
On life's Hardway Road.

The Nature of Patriotism.

Given the immense personal sacrifices which were required in order that the English nation state might come into existence, my mind turned to the nature of patriotism. I asked myself, what is it exactly? How does it reveal itself? It is a question of course, which is not exclusive to the English.

As an Englishman by birth and nature, I began by asking myself, 'am I a patriot?' I was rather surprised therefore, when the answer came back, 'no.'

I found this difficult to believe. As a child I was brought up in the post war period. All the adults I knew had taken part in the war. My parents, teachers, shop keepers, everyone. As I grew up and understood the sacrifices that had been made on my behalf, I became more appreciative of the role they had played. In my mind, I was quite clear that were I presented with similar circumstances, then I would do as they, and the men and boys of the Hardway Road had done. I would fight the barbarians. Not just because it was my patriotic duty, but on a common sense level, when the wolf is at the door, you may as well go down fighting, as sit in a supine stupor, awaiting your grisly fate.

So as you can imagine, my response left me a little confused. I considered the idea, that perhaps I didn't know myself as well as I thought. A strange idea, because I have known myself ever since I began life as a small foetus. Though you must forgive me if I don't regal you with tales of life spent in the amniotic fluid, as events around that time are a little hazy. But the main point here is, that after a lengthy consideration, I slowly and by degrees, began to get a handle on patriotism. In particular, the nature of it and how it reveals itself.

I came to the conclusion that patriotism operates in the manner of a light bulb. It is either on, or it is off. Essentially, it is only switched on when the situation demands. So when I had asked myself, was I a patriot? The reason I said no, was because there was no immediate threat which required that I should be patriotic. There was no wolf at the door and no immediately accessible crisis. So the light switch remained off.

Similarly, when patriotism is viewed as a power, it is I fancy, akin to the power that lays hidden within a magic charm. It lays dormant, unmoved by the world about it, until such time as events conspire to raise it from its quiescent state. At that moment, it springs to life and shines a light in the darkness and shows the road that one must travel. In a practical sense, it also shines a light on those whose patriotism is not to their fellow man and woman, but to their own greed and avarice.

So for me, patriotism is all about the moment. If you are a political leader or business man of high influence, it is how you react when a decision affecting the rights and freedoms of your country men and women is put before you. Do you make the decision that is best and honourable for them? Or do you accept the cash inducements which are quietly offered via a series of nudges, winks, and funny handshakes?

It is in that moment, and only that moment, that you find the true heart. For patriotism emerges only from those who are true of heart. Those that believe in a greater good, beyond their own self advancement.

That's when the magic springs to life. That's when you find out, those for whom it burns brightly, and those for whom there is nothing within but a self-entitled black hole.

We saw during and post the Brexit debate that our political classes are largely bereft of patriotism. There is the issue of allowing a globalist corporation like the European Union to take control of our borders. Then there is the decades long betrayal of allowing Viking raiders to plunder fish from our waters and by extension, food from our plates.

These are the acts of betrayal which reveal the sly treachery of our political classes.

Alfred suffered from this betrayal when he barely escaped with his life in Christmas 878.

It was the same people; wealthy 'noble' men,' and self-worshipping idolaters, like the Arch bishop of Canterbury, who moved with a nudge here and a wink there, to pave the way for their new barbarian chums.

Nothing much has changed since then, because human psychology remains unchanged.

As a final note on patriotism, I would add that I am completely unimpressed with society's 'professional' patriots. I refer here, to those who project patriotism 24 hours a day, seven days a week. Show me one of those, and I will show you a very tedious fellow.

Having said that, show me someone who is never patriotic and I will show you someone who is never to be trusted. In England, you can easily spot those people, because they like to pour vitriol wherever they abound; and they act in similar fashion to that of Dracula, who flinches at the sign of the cross. Similar in their own way to Dracula, these home grown, spiritually dead malevolents, recoil at the sight of the Union Flag.

I can perfectly understand why this is so. The Union Flag came into being as an expression of the unity between tribes who had once waged war upon each other. Where spiritually inclined folk see a symbol of unity, the sly malevolants recoil in horror. They are society's, spiritual apostates.

Incidentally:

Union, has a dna of, 1.

Unity, a dna of, 8.

Love of country, a dna of, Master Number 11.

It's My Party.
(And I'll lie if I want to).

Part of the problem we face in modern English society, is that the two major political monstrosities – Labour and Conservative – have by degrees, corrupted their political updates. In this matter they are little different to software providers, who from time to time, update their program or operating system and in the process, have taken out those bits we found most useful and pleasing. Both Conservative and Labour, have done much the same thing.

In particular, their system updates have taken out the patriotic elements and the sense of kinship with their fellow country men and women, and replaced it with an obsequious desire to embrace cronyism, multi corporate prosperity, and the teachings of the false God Mammon.

Let's take a quick snapshot of that most wretched organisation, The Conservative Party. They use to be the party of the Union, but that element got removed – in a spiritual sense – during one of their 'progressive' system updates.

It is often difficult to pinpoint in exact terms when things go awry, as decay is a gradual process; it moves slowly, which in turn, allows adjustments to be made, until by degrees, those adjustments become the accepted norm. But a good place to start is the United Kingdom's entry into the European Union (or European Economic Community. EEC as it was once named) in 1973.

Entry of itself, was neither a good nor bad thing. The problem was the terms of entry. It was the terms of entry which incubated the traitor gene within the Conservative political soul and it is this, which in turn set them on the path to the mendacious ruin we see today.

During the Second World War, the country was struggling to feed itself. It was thanks in part to our brave fishermen, who went into dangerous seas, in order to harvest a vital foodstuff which helped the Nation through difficult times.

Many were lost – particularly in the early years from 1941 to 42. Estimates suggest, that up to 1,300 of these brave souls went to a watery grave as a result of bombings and machine gun fire.

All this meant little to the traitors in the Conservative high command, who thought nothing of giving away our fishing rights to overseas adventurers, and in the process, allowing food to be stolen off the nations plates. They had already performed a similar trick two years earlier, when the Education Minister, Margaret Thatcher, had stolen free school milk from the Nation's children, and in the process had earned the sobriquet, 'Milk Snatcher Thatcher.'

Entry to the European Economic Community also dealt a savage financial blow to members of the Commonwealth like: Australia, New Zealand and Canada, who now faced tariffs on the foodstuffs and other items which they exported to us.

These were countries which during the war had sent young men to fight with us. Many of those young men would never return. The wretched creature which was the Conservative Party, was indifferent to such niceties. If you are going to steal food off the plates of your fellow man and woman, and snatch milk from the mouths of their children, then spitting in the face of those from places far away, is but the work of a quick moment.

The Labour Party by contrast, had not – unlike the Conservatives – performed the system update which had removed the patriotic element of their operating system. They were – by and large – opposed to entry on these terms. In this respect they were still the patriotic socialist party that had come to power in the post war period.

This post war party led by Clement Atlee, was in its own way a 20th Century version of the 'post' Viking administration, led by the patriotic socialist, Alfred The Great.

Like Alfred, the post war Labour Government had quickly set about rebuilding a nation turned to rubble. Like Alfred, they had stood shoulder to shoulder with their comrades through common dangers and privations. They had their failings – as does every organisation – but stealing food from the plates of the workers and milk from children, was not as yet on their agenda.

Scroll forward some 25 years to the introduction of the new Tony Blair Operating System, and you can see that with this new system update, that patriotic socialism had been removed from Labour. It had been replaced with more efficient methods of delivering the delinquent mendacities that had proved so ruinous under Conservative regimes. Though for traditionalists, they still offered elements of the classic view, which came in the form of key words and phrases in a speech; slogans on a billboard; and the inclusion in the cabinet of at least one old style traditionalist, who whilst never permitted input into major policy decisions, was essential for ornamental purposes, and as a sop to appease the true hearts.

It was under the Tony Blair system update, that the war monger patch (TB 2.0) was introduced. This new patch, which the Labour Party had previously thought unnecessary and unwholesome, acted as a search engine, whose primary function was to seek out new lands and new peoples on whom they could rain death and destruction.

During the TB tenure, death and destruction was rained down on people in such diverse places as:

Iraq 1998. Kosovo 1999. Afghanistan 2000. And Iraq (the sequel) in 2003.

It is interesting to note that in 2003, so keen was this Labour administration to bring death and destruction to an Arab nation, nearly 3000 miles away, that they cooked up a dossier of falsehoods in order to legitimise their need for bloodlust.

No wonder many people in many parts of the world hate us. I don't blame them. I would also hate us.

It hardly needs mentioning, that the Conservative Party was very supportive of such action. In common with the New TB 2.0 Labour Party, the Conservatives saw no wrongdoing in killing people en masse, on distant parts of the planet. Also, unlike the Army of The Hardway Road under Alfred's stewardship, and unlike the unified command structure of the Allied Forces in the second world war, these modern day warriors, stayed safe at home in cosy apartments, while others were doing the dirty work for them.

If we scroll forward to 2024, we can see that further refinements had been made to the respective operating platforms of both, The Labour and Conservative Party.

In 2024 the Conservatives had been in power for 14 years. During which time they had trashed the economy. Failed to carry out their promises. Allowed all aspects of the cultural and industrial and financial and social fabric of the country to fall into a state of disrepair. Had allowed sewage to pour into our rivers and water ways, and in doing so, had demonstrated – as if demonstration was required – that there was a sewer running through their soul.

But if that wasn't enough, they had during this period, awarded themselves some 64 Knighthoods and Damehoods; and former Prime Minister Boris Johnsonn had given a Lordship to his brother.

So to some – like myself – the stink of self-entitlement has about it the whiff of the sewage farm. But to smug collectors of ill-deserved honours, it would appear that a sewage farm is a place rich in fragrant smells.

Within months of coming to power in the 2024 Election victory, the new Prime Minister Sir Keir Starmer announced, 'those with the broadest shoulders should bear the heavier burden.'

That rather contradicted the fact that he had taken the winter fuel allowance from pensioners. Also, his party had done next to nothing to stop the child abuse cases in Labour controlled constituencies; and whilst in post as Leader of the opposition, he had supported the

Conservative party Prime Minister in hiving off the administration of Northern Island to an administrative quango in Brussels and supported the Conservatives in their long standing antipathy to our fishing communities and complete indifference to matters of national interest. He had also been keen to give away sovereignty of the Chagos Islands without seeking the permission of the people whose property it was. Hardly surprising, because tyrants don't seek permission; they impose their will.

So the once patriotic socialist Labour Party had now fully embraced the sewer values of the Conservative Party. Where once there were two, now there was one. Between them, they had become: The Great Stink!

Burgess	**Philby**
Blunt	**Maclean**
Conservative	**Labour**

A Tale of Two Leaders.

1). Alfred fought one war on home soil in defence of his country. Blair never fought a war in defence of his country. 2). Alfred fought against a foreign invader. Blair always was the foreign invader. 3). In battle, Alfred led from the front. When a photo opportunity presented itself, Blair stood at the front. 4). Alfred embraced the common people. Blair embraced the rich and powerful. 5). Alfred put the socialism in Government. Blair sucked it out. 6).One of them, was a Great Socialist King. The other, a rather tawdry sort of a chap.

The (Spiritual) Battle Songs
of The Hardway Road.

Over the next few pages are the lyrics and back ground information of the songs I wrote, and which make up the (Spiritual) Battle Songs of the Hardway Road.

There is an eclectic mix – which is good – because it means there's something for everyone; (and plenty for those of a miserable disposition to moan about).

So I make no apology for my inclusive nature. Those who are anti inclusive – like for example the anti-inclusive degenerates who take away working peoples bank accounts or block their social media accounts – can do one!

Together in Starlight. (Dna 1)

This is the English National Anthem. It has its spiritual roots in the Hardway Road, and its verses echo the mood and landscape of the boys and men who walked together along its moonlit track, towards an uncertain future.

It has two versions. One is an upbeat – put on your dancing shoes – version, for sporting occasions, such as when the England football team are in the field.

The Cathedral version, is sung without the chorus and at a slower tempo, for those more reflective occasions.

The full version was written partly in response to the Italian and French national anthems. I love those anthems. The French one starts off at 100 miles an hour and just keeps accelerating. The Italian one has a very enjoyable bounce up and down quality.

For me, God Save the King/Queen isn't quite appropriate, not least because it is the British UK National Anthem. Whereas, Together in Starlight is the true English National Anthem; because in the space of a little over a minute, it tells not only the story of England, but more important than that, it celebrates the unsung working class heroes who were fundamental to its birth. (Power to the People).

Also – and this is purely a personal opinion – I wanted something with a tempo that could go toe to toe with the French and Italian anthems.

I don't for one moment claim that, Together in Starlight is as good or better than the par excellence of the French or Italian anthems; but it does have that, 'put on your dancing shoes' quality. Also, the three titles have something in common. 'Together in Starlight' has a dna of 1. As does, 'La Marseillaise' and 'Inno di Mameli' (Mameli's Hymn) which is one of the three titles by which the Italian National anthem is known. (The other two are 'il Canto degli Italiani' the song of the Italians and 'Fratelli d'Italia,' brothers of Italy).

It is also worth noting, that in addition to the title, that the lyrics of the full version of Together in Starlight, also have a combined dna of 1. So there is a certain spiritual symmetry there and its dna reflects the dna of the name Alfred, which is also 1.

Note: at the time of going to print, the Football Association appointed the German national, Thomas Tuchel, as England manager. The name, 'Thomas Tuchel,' has a numerological dna of 1. So he may have a German passport, but his dna is in sync with the English National Anthem. So on a spiritual level, he is very much a 'Starlight Football Tommy.'

On a personal level, I am also very proud of the fact that England have never lost a cup final when, Together in Starlight has been played.

Eagle in The Sky.

The under laying theme of this song is: that circumstances will often conspire to put us into a dark place. I have been in those places myself, particularly in my younger days when I was homeless. But no matter how impoverished our circumstances, or how dark the approaching storm clouds, we can always find the strength of will to rise above the hardships which confront us.(The lyrics have a combined numerological value of, **dna 8**).

Stand Up And Fight For England. (dna 8)

This is the kind of song which I can easily imagine that football fans from other nations would take enormous delight in removing the word England from the chorus line, and substituting it with their own nations name; and then having done that, singing it back to us after their team has given us a good thrashing.

You might think that as the author of the song, this would annoy me. You would be completely wrong. I have a dry sense of humour, and things like that I find quietly hilarious. Besides which, everyone adapts songs to suit their own needs and moods. It is part of human nature. You borrow our song, we appropriate yours. What goes around comes around. Besides which, I don't believe in the phoney concept of cultural appropriation. If I did, then I would insist that the nations of the world shut down their industries and return to their agrarian roots. Let us not forget, it was the British who invented the Industrial Revolution. Industry is part of our culture. So if you're one of these phonies who believe that embracing elements of another nation's culture is a sin, then I suggest you start with that industrialised sin, and then work your way back to the stone age where you belong.

The Girls Go Woo Woo. (Dna 1)

This is the battle song for women on a girly night out. I think in general terms, women carry a greater burden through life than men. Pregnancy is the most obvious example, though dealing with men is very much the problem hiding in plain sight.

With regards to pregnancy, it not only places a physical strain, but it can interrupt their career choices. Also with a baby in the house, it can turn their brains fuzzy and produce weird speech patterns, which generate a high pitched wonky sound. So this song is for those occasions when they are with their girl pals, and for a short while they can forget their many responsibilities and enjoy themselves in a Woo Woo friendly environment.

Incidentally, not only does the title of the song have a dna of 1, but the chorus line, **'and you know the girls have got their Woo Woo On,'** also has a dna of 1. So whichever way you look at it, the women of the world are established at number 1 in the charts.

So well done Mrs. Woman. And for the curious minded, **'Mrs Woman'** has a dna of **8**. **'Women Are Great,'** has a dna of **1**; and **'Mrs. People,'** a dna of Master Number **11**.

IMPORTANT NOTICE.

There is an instrumental version of this song which is scientifically calibrated to test the strength of any woman's, Woo Woo. Those women who wish to self-test, are required to sit down in a high back chair facing their computer, music centre or other such audio player. This having been accomplished, they then press the play button. If the Woo Woo flows through them, their shoulders will begin to move from left to right in time with the music. Soon after, their arms and hands will follow suit. Then if the Woo Woo is strong within them, they will rise up and dance to the rhythm of the Woo Woo, as if they were a show girl, who is wearing a gold pineapple on her head. **May The Woo Woo Be With You!**

Women of England

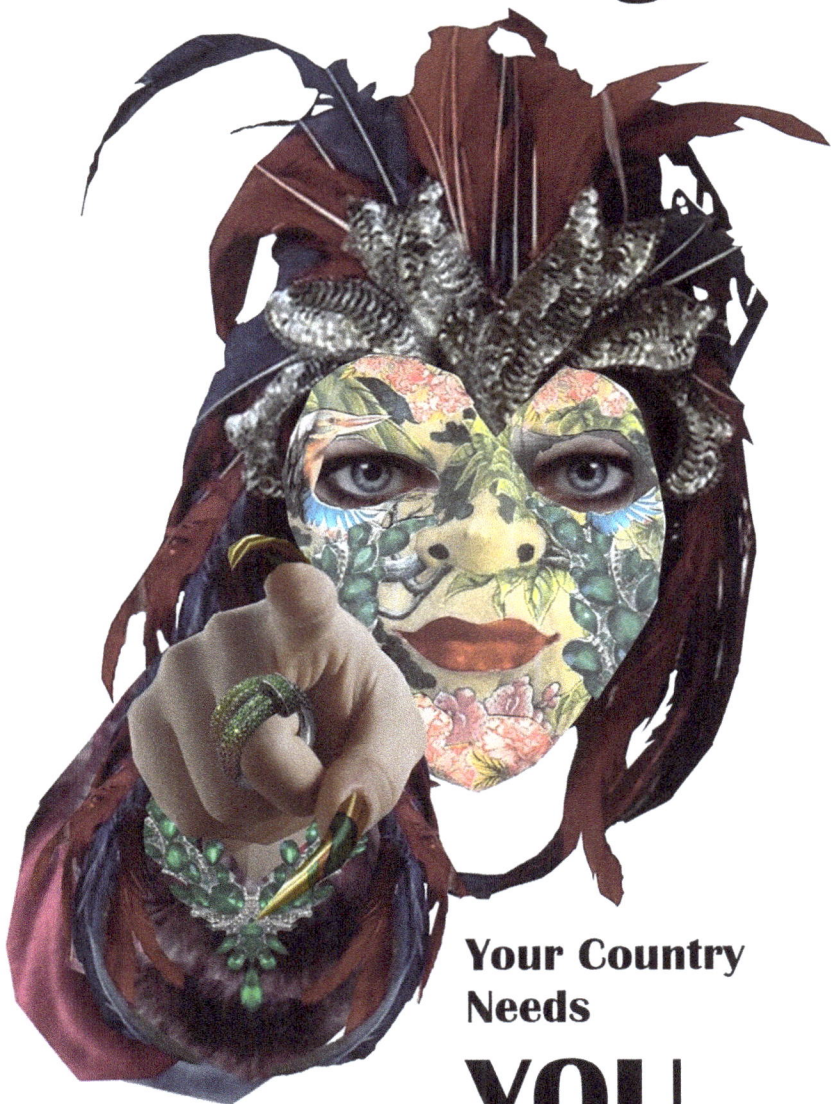

**Your Country
Needs**

YOU

The Big Boys Pants. (Dna 11)

We live in a world where everyone likes to think they are a tough guy. This song is a celebration of that fact. In my mind, I see it sitting alongside, YMCA by the Village People, as a celebration of tough guy masculinity. In fact, if you alter the opening line of YMCA to read, 'young man I was once in your pants,' then the two songs are conjoined in a celebration of heterosexual manhood.

Another point about this song, which some may find interesting, is how it came into being.

Very often, the creative process is a product of hidden forces which rise up mysteriously from the depths of our subconscious, leaving in their wake no trail by which we may follow it back to the source.

So often times, ideas arrive seemingly from nowhere and are given substance by an author, artist or engineer.

On this particular occasion, I knew where the idea came from and how it all fell into place. I was trying to fit the word, gold lamé (pronounced: lar-may) into another song I had written. Sadly for me, I couldn't do it.

(Note: Lamé is a brocaded clothing fabric made from metallic fibres. It is one of those fabrics which give off a tinsel effect, much beloved of tough guys strutting their stuff).

So I was sitting their scratching my head, when a man on the radio by the name of Simon Jordan, suggested that a certain football team, who were showing a lack of fight, needed to get their **big boy pants on.'**

For people who don't know who Simon Jordan is: he's a quietly spoken business man who once owned Crystal Palace Football Club. He currently – at the time of writing – has a spot on Talk Sport radio station, where he dispenses pearls of wisdom to an enlightened audience. He is by nature a modest man, who in the normal course of events would like nothing more than to hide his light under a bushel.

Unfortunately – as he would be quick to tell you – due to climate change, the bushel forests aren't as big as they once were and as a consequence, he is unable to find a bushel large enough to hide the lamp of his genius.

But in any event, it was his discourse on the benefits of a big boys pants regime as a route to footballing success, which generated the creative spark that fertilised my tinselly mind set, and which in turn, produced the song which is a lyrical paean to tough guys everywhere.

So in effect, this song was a product of two men.

Simon Jordan's intellectual loins, and my artistic womb.

While I think about it, a thought has just occurred to me. There is another tough guy song which I forgot to mention. That song is of course, 'Yes sir, I can Boogie,' by Baccara.

So just to clarify, there are now 3 top of the range, tough guy songs out there.

They are:

'Yes Sir, I can Boogie.' (Baccara)

'YMCA.' (Village People)

And now with great fanfare (and such trousered adjustments as are necessary to facilitate ballroom dancing); I give to the world….

'The Big Boys Pants.'

Welcome To You. (dna 1)

This song began life as a merger. On the one hand I was listening to a radio presenter called, Shebhan Ahern. Listening to her, I thought, 'that's a tricky sausage of a name to work into a song.'

I mean, it's not like:

'I want to marry Sally O'Malley, the girl who lives down the street in Dilly Dally Alley.'

A name like Sally, just trips off the tongue.

Shebahn, requires a little more thought.

And at the very same time that I was wrestling with that particular lyrical conundrum, I was also trying to conjure up some lyrics for a song which children might enjoy singing.

When I was a small boy at school, we had weekly sing songs in the classroom. I always enjoyed them. We all did. So somehow – I'm not sure how – the two ideas merged into a cheery song of welcome; and as a bonus, the title of the song had a numerological **dna of 1.**

(Which was nice).

So for anyone listening to it, I would recommend that you imagine it being sung by a group of school children who are welcoming a distinguished visitor to the school. The school teacher who is conducting proceedings, is wearing a fixed smile on her face, because she is worried that the trouble makers in the back row are going to act up.

Do that, and you will be in the right head space to appreciate the song. Then maybe, like myself, you will be transported back in time to the classroom you yourself once sat in. And it may be the case, that like me, you yourself were one of the back row trouble makers.

It's Birthday Time. (dna 11)

This final song might be of interest to those people who like to support a good cause, because I have donated all financial rights from the song to: the NSPCC. (National Society for The prevention of Cruelty to Children).

We live in a world where people are forever espousing some good cause or other. Often times, the 'good cause' on offer, is nothing more than a vehicle by which self- important narcissus can showcase their virtue to the world.

'Look at me, aren't I wonderful,' they're saying.

Many of these causes, and the individuals who promote them are as substantial as the clothes which the Emperor wore in Hans Christian Anderson's book,'The Emperor's New Clothes.'

But for me, the most vulnerable group in the world, are children. A two year who is being abused, can't rock up to the offices of his local Member of Parliament and ask for help. They need others to speak up for them. Yet when was the last time you saw angry demonstrators on the street, agitating on their behalf ?

The streets are full of posers, vandalising buildings and monuments, but there doesn't appear to be a public appetite to take to the streets in support of the one group in society which truly needs our support.

The song I wrote, is entitled, **It's Birthday Time.**

It is a simple alternative to Happy Birthday.

So in this world of streaming services and downloads, then I would respectfully suggest that **whenever** you go on to your favourite music download site, that the first thing you do, is download, **It's Birthday Time.** It will only take a second and all the royalties will go to the NSPCC.

Similarly, if you are on a radio or TV station do the same. If you just play it once every now and then, that that will add funds to the cause. Then when you go to bed at night, you can do so in the knowledge that you have done a very good thing.

Life can be very complicated at times, but here is a solution to a problem which only requires the touch of a button.

Go on.

Press that button.

Download it.

You know you want to.

It's Birthday Time.
It's birthday time for you.
We love you, yes we do.
It's birthday time,
It's birthday time;
We love you,
Yes, we do...
Happy Birthday!

Together in Starlight. (dna 1)

Let brightest starlight,
Watch over me.
A celestial candle,
In a timeless sea.

Let none despair,
When all seems lost.
We'll share the burden,
We'll bear the cost.

On Lonely pathways,
Through moonlit fields.
A ghostly army,
To none we yield.

We travelled far,
On a Hardway Road.
We made light work,
Of a heavy load.

So far away,
Or near at home.
To far flung places,
Where ere we roam.
I am England,
First and last.
Can you hear the beat?
Of a lion heart.

Can you hear the beat?
Can you hear the beat?
Of a lion heart.

(Huzzah! Huzzah! Huzzah!)

Eagle In The Sky.

(Alfred's Song).

When dawns light is breaking,
And the sleepy night gives way to the day.
As the sun is rising,
Like falling snow my troubles melt away.
Though my sad heart be broken,
My spirit survives.
In my mind I'm a free bird,
And I fly like an eagle in the sky.

As I sail across life's ocean,
I don't dwell on things that might have been.
I look, to the future,
For there lays might heart, my hope, my dreams.
Though dark clouds assail me,
My spirit survives.
In my mind I'm a free bird,
And I fly like an eagle in the sky.
And I fly like an eagle in the sky.

Stand Up And Fight For England. (dna 8)

Stand up and fight for England,
True heart will see me through.
Stand up and fight for England,
You know what you must do.

Keep the faith.
Don't give in.
When you fight,
You fight, to win win win.
With heart of oak.
With charm and wit.
With style and professorship,
Ho!
Stand up and Fight for England,
Till freedoms dream comes true.

In days of yore,
We lived our lives;
In fear of Viking seas.
But we didn't bow long,
To the Danelaw con,
And our spirit set us free.

So keep the faith.
Don't give in.
When you fight; you fight to,
Win Win Win.
Stand up and fight for England,
Till freedoms dream comes true.
Till freedoms dream comes true.

(Huzzah! Huzzah! Huzzah!)

The Girls Go Woo Woo. (dna 1)

Let the party begin!
When you hear the hoots and giggles,
And the samba hips and wiggles;
It's fun time at the party festival.
And when the noise is slowly rising,
It's hardly that surprising;
And You know the girls have got their Woo Woo On.
Woo Woo On!

When they move, they own the samba,
The tango and the bosa nova too.
With their high kick feats,
And show girl moves;
They're always in a show girl mood,
And You know the girls have got their Woo Woo On.
Woo Woo On!
And You know the girls have got their Woo Woo on.
Woo Woo On!

No one, does the Woo Woo better,
Woo Woo!
They are the fun time funsters in the world.
In the world!
And with the tempo, quickly rising,
You know the sound of love is in the air.
In the air!
And when they set,
The dance floor spinning.
They're in the groove,
They've made their move,
And You know the girls have got their Woo Woo On.
Woo Woo On!

And You know the girls have got their Woo Woo On.
Woo Woo On!
And You know the girls have got their Woo Woo on.
Woo Woo On!

Shake those hips.
Pucker those lips.
A quick two step,
Do the ballet high kicks.

And You know the girls have got their Woo Woo On.
Woo Woo On!
Wooooooo ooo Wooooooo ooo Wooooooo ooo!

The Big Boys Pants. (dna 11)

Get your gold bling on,
Straighten up your tie.
It's big boy pants time,
I'm telling no lie.

Because, we're doing the big boy,
Doing the big boy.
Doing the big boy, pants;
Go Pilates!

Doing the big boy,
Doing the big boy,
Doing the big boy;
Dancing in our speedos.

Cos that's what big boys do;
Please believe me.

That's what big boys do;
In gold lamé

That's what big boys do;
Going Bangla.

Because, Big Boys,
Wear big pants.
Youzza Baby!

It's so what,
Big Boys do.
Tutti Frutti!

And Big Boys,
Oooby doooby doo.
Like a diva!

And Big Boys,
Oooby dooby.
Dooby dooby,

Booby dooby;
Oooby dooby,
Doooby dooby
Doooby…Doo…bee…
Dooooooooooo
(Cocka doodle dooo..)

Welcome To You. (dna 1)

Welcome to you.
Welcome to you.
Everybody sing and dance,
Sing, welcome to you.
Aye!

Once a wee Glasgow lass,
Shebhan was her name.
She sang and danced,
Upon the stage,
Is how she came to fame.
And everyone who saw her there,
From Glasgow to Bahrain.
They put on their dancing shoes,
When ere they heard her name.
Aye!
(Chorus)

Welcome to you.
Welcome to you.
Everybody sing and dance,
Sing, welcome to you.

They say this is a magic song,
It brightens every room.
It turns away despairing thoughts,
And banishes the gloom.

So if you will,
Like Turtle doves,
And courting couples do.
Please sing this song of joyful note,
With a coochy coochy coo.
Aye!
(Chorus)

Welcome to you.
Welcome to you.
Everybody sing and dance,
Sing, welcome to you.

Welcome to you.
Welcome to you.
Everybody sing and dance,
Sing, welcome to you.

We always sing this little song,
Through sunshine, wind or rain.
We never get downhearted,
Our spirits never wane;
And all because this happy song,
Tells what we all must do.
I think you know the answer;
Sing, welcome to you.
Aye!
(Chorus)

Welcome to you.
Welcome to you.
Everybody sing and dance,
Sing, welcome to you.

Welcome to you.
(Tempo slowing).
Welcome to yoooo…
Everybody sing and dance,
(Tempo slows to a halt.).
Sing, welcome to,
Yooooo……ooo…ooooh!

On Causing Upset.

Whilst writing this tome, I have – from time to time – expressed a personal view. If having read some of my personal views, it has moved some of you to form an instant dislike of me, then I have to say I am highly delighted by this turn of events.

Taking an instant dislike to someone is perfectly normal. It's nothing to be ashamed of. That is because there are some 8 billion or so people in the world. You can't like them all, nor they you. It is a feature of human psychology. We all do it, and mostly it is a completely harmless exercise.

From time to time I will see someone online or on a televisual device, and for reasons I can never truly understand, I will immediately form a negative opinion of them. (The opposite is also very much true).

So the fact that some of you may now have begun forming a negative opinion of me, is completely heart-warming.

The reason I am so very pleased with this recent development, is because I feel that working together like this – with me putting out negative views to someone over there, and with you putting out your negative views to me over here – that we are, in some small way, helping to keep the Universe in balance; and keeping the Universe in balance is something which is very important to me.

The universe is a big place, and keeping it in balance is not something I can do all by myself. I need your help. I need you to rally round me in my hour of need.

So to all those people who don't like me…

Thanks buddy.

You're the best.

This tome is ended.
Thank you for your company;
Goodbye and God bless.

www.ingramcontent.com/pod-product-compliance
Lightning Source LLC
LaVergne TN
LVHW010316070426
835513LV00021B/2405